Our Faith and Worship

A Textbook of Islamic *'Aqā'id* and *'Arkān*

Elementary Level
Grade Three and Four

New Revised and Expanded Edition

Vol. I

Dr. Abidullah Ghazi
Dr. Tasneema K. Ghazi

IQRA'
INTERNATIONAL EDUCATIONAL FOUNDATION
CHICAGO, IL. USA

Part of a Comprehensive and Systematic Program of Islamic Studies

A Textbook for the Program of *'Aqīdah* and *Fiqh* Elementary Level

Our Faith and Worship Vol.1

Chief Program Editors
Dr. Abidullah al-Ansari Ghazi
(Ph.D., Study of Religion
Harvard University)

Dr. Tasneema Ghazi
(Ph.D., Curriculum-Reading
University of Minnesota)

Language Editing
Noura Durkee
Fadel Abdallah
Huseyin Abiva

Reviewed by
Shaikh Muhammad
Noor Abdullah
Ph.D., University of Chicago

Shaikh Abdullah Saleem
Fadil, Dar ul-Ulum, Deoband

International Institute of
Islamic Thought
Department of Education

Typesetting
Wajeeha Ansari
Nasr Khan Kunwar

Design
Jennifer Mazzoni
B..A. Illustration,
Columbia College Chicago
Cover Illustration:
Blue Mosque, Istanbul Turkey

Illustrations
Mahnaz Karimi

Re Design
Aliuddin Khaja

Revised & Expanded Edition
Sixth Printing in U.S.A. September, 2007

Library of Congress Catalog Card Number 94-65596
ISBN # 1-56316-055-2

Dedication

My maternal grandfather
Sayyid Shah Muhammad Miyan (d. 1957),
whose loving arms were my first Madrasah.
May Allah bless him with Jannah.

Dr. Abidullah Ghazi

لا إله إلا الله
محمد رسول الله

A NOTE TO PARENTS AND TEACHERS

We are honored to present to you this new expanded and revised edition of Our Faith and Worship, Volume I. Based on the suggestions and recommendations of many teachers and parents, we have added five new lesson on Islamic *'Akhlāq* in this edition.

This textbook has been is written for grades three and four as part of IQRA's comprehensive and systematic program of *'Aqidah, Fiqh* and *'Akhlāq*. This volume covers most of the important questions dealing with *'Aqidah, Ṣalāh* and *'Akhlāq* at age appropriate reading levels. The second volume of Our Faith and Worship deals with *Ṣaum, Zakāh, Ḥajj* as well as *'Akhlāq*. Textbooks written for the junior and senior levels deal with the same subjects at a higher level and in greater details.

'Aqidah, Fiqh and *'Akhlāq* are three of the most important topics which must be appropriately covered at each grade level in the curriculum of Islamic Studies. *'Aqidah* deals with the Islamic belief system which is founded on *Tawḥid* (Oneness of God) and *Risalah* (the prophethood of Muhammad ﷺ). *Fiqh* deals with all questions relating to *'Ibadat* (rituals) and *Mu'amlat* (social dealings). *'Akhlāq* teaches us Islamic values and manners.

It is all the more important to teach *'Aqidah, Fiqh* and *'Akhlāq* to children and youth in this pluralistic and expanding world where religious, cultural, rational and materialistic ideas often compete with the moral teachings that have shaped Islamic life for centuries. IQRA's educational program fills the gap which exists in the teachings of Islam to young Muslims at their own levels of understanding through well prepared materials.

The revised program of *'Aqidah, Fiqh* and *'Akhlāq* has been prepared for each grade of elementary and junior high levels. Our textbooks and workbooks are prepared by well-known scholars and educators. Workbooks are an essential part of IQRA's educational efforts and must be used for best results and creative teaching.

We request all teachers and parents to inform us of their opinions and suggestions. We shall gratefully accept positive suggestions and improve the text and enhance its usefulness, *In-shā'-Allah.*

IQRA's efforts at producing quality Islamic educational material has been acknowledged in educational circles around the world. IQRA's educational material is now being used in Islamic schools throughout North America and in many other countries. It is being translated into some of the world's major languages.

We are grateful to Allah ﷻ for this humble success and appeal to all concerned individuals to make special *Du'ā'* for IQRA' and participate in this Islamic educational work.

It is through our joint endeavors that we can build IQRA' International Educational Foundation as a viable and professional Islamic educational institution. May Allah ﷻ help us to fulfill this mission.

The Chief Editors

Table of Contents

Lesson 1

OUR RELIGION IS ISLAM

We are Muslims and our religion is Islam.
Our *Shahādah* is:

أَشْهَدُ أَنْ لاَ إِلَهَ إِلاَّ اللَّهُ ،
وَأَشْهَدُ أَنَّ مُحَمَّدًا رَسُولُ اللَّهِ

'Ashhadu 'an la 'ilāha 'ill-Allāhu
I bear witness there is no god but Allah,
Wa 'Ashhadu 'anna Muhammadan-Rasūlullāh
And I bear witness that Muhammad is the Messenger of Allah.

Shahādah means, "To bear witness". Those who make this *Shahādah* and believe in it are called Muslims.

The word "Islam" comes from the Arabic word *Salima,* which means peace. Islam is a religion of peace.

The word Islam also comes from another Arabic word *Aslama,* which means to obey. Islam is a religion of obedience to Allah ﷻ. Allah ﷻ says in the Qur'an:

وَرَضِيتُ لَكُمُ ٱلْإِسْلَـٰمَ دِينًا

I have chosen for you Islam as the religion.
(*Al - Mā'idah* 5:3)

A Muslim is one who believes in Islam as his religion and follows its teachings.
A Muslim is one who believes in Allah ﷻ as his Lord and Creator.
A Muslim is one who obeys the teachings of the Qur'ān.
A Muslim is one who follows Muhammad ﷺ as the final Prophet and Messenger.

All Muslims are one *'Ummah*. *'Ummah* means a community or a nation. The Muslim *'Ummah* means that all the Muslims are one community of believers. All Muslims have common beliefs and all of them follow the teachings of Islam.

Muslims are not one race, they are not of one color, and they do not speak the same language. But all Muslims are one *'Ummah*, one community. All Muslims are brothers and sisters to one another.

Muslims live all over the world. Muslims are black, white, yellow and brown. There are more than one billion Muslims in the world. One out of every five persons living in the world is a Muslim.

There are millions of Muslims living in North America. Islam is the fastest growing religion in the world. All Muslims are equal before Allah ﷻ. No one among them is superior to others.

The *Qur'ān* says:

إِنَّ أَكْرَمَكُمْ عِندَ اللَّهِ أَتْقَاكُمْ

The best in the eyes of Allah is one who is most pious.
(*'Al-Hujurat* 49:13)

We thank Allah ﷻ for giving us His religion, Islam. We thank Allah ﷻ for sending us His book, the Qur'ān. We thank Allah ﷻ for choosing us to be in the *'Ummah* of Prophet Muhammad ﷺ.

WE HAVE LEARNED:

- Islam means a religion of peace and obedience to Allah.
- Those who follow Islam are called Muslims.
- All the Muslims are one *'Ummah* (community). We are brothers and sisters to each other.

DO WE KNOW THESE WORDS?

'Aslama, Islam, obedience, *Salima, Shahādah*, to bear witness, *'Ummah.*

Lesson 2

THE BELIEFS OF MUSLIMS

All Muslims have common beliefs. All Muslims must know these beliefs; they must say them with their tongues and accept them in their hearts.

Such a belief is called *'Imān Mufassal,* the Complete Faith. Let us learn *'Imān Mufassal*, in both Arabic and English and understand its meaning.

آمَنْتُ بِاللهِ وَمَلائِكَتِهِ وَكُتُبِهِ وَرُسُلِهِ ،
وَالْيَوْمِ الآخِرِ ،
وَالْقَدَرِ خَيْرِهِ وَشَرِّهِ مِنَ اللهِ تَعَالَى ،
وَالْبَعْثِ بَعْدَ الْمَوْتِ

'Amantu bi-Llāhi wa malā'ikati-hi wa kutubi-hi, wa rusuli-hi
I believe in Allah, and in His Angels, and in His Books, and in His Messengers,
wa-l-yawmil -'ākhiri
and in the Last Day,
wal-qadari khairi-hi wa sharri-hi min-Allāhi Ta'ālā
and in the *Qadar* (the Power) to do good or bad is from Allah, the High
wal-ba'thi ba'd al-mawt.
and in the life after death.

All Muslims believe in One God, Who is our Lord and Creator. Allah سبحانه وتعالى has created angels from *Nūr*, light, to serve Him and worship Him. He chose Angel Jibril عليه السلام to bring His Books to the Prophets.

Allah سبحانه وتعالى has sent many Books to lead humankind to the path of Islam. Allah سبحانه وتعالى has sent many Prophets and Messengers to guide people to the true path of Islam.

One day we will die, but Allah ﷻ will bring us back to life on the Last Day, the Day of Judgment. Allah ﷻ is All-Powerful and He controls everything. Whatever good or bad happens in this world is with His permission. There is a life after death which will last forever. Believing in all of these points makes one a Muslim.

In the next chapters we shall explain these articles of Muslim faith.

WE HAVE LEARNED:

- All Muslims have common beliefs.
- A Muslim must believe in all of them.
- We must memorize *'Imān Mufassal* and learn its meaning.

DO WE KNOW THESE WORDS?

Article, Day of Judgment, *'Imān Mufassal*, *Nūr*, permission.

Lesson 3

BELIEF IN ALLAH سبحانه وتعالى

Muslims believe that there is no god but Allah سبحانه وتعالى , the One God . Allah سبحانه وتعالى has created everything. He controls everything. We belong to Allah سبحانه وتعالى and to Him is our return.

Allah سبحانه وتعالى has created angels, *Jinns* and humans. Allah سبحانه وتعالى created the sky, the sun, the moon and the stars. He created the animals, the birds and the fish.

Allah سبحانه وتعالى makes the trees grow. He makes the flowers bloom. He makes the fruits ripen.

He has made the oceans, clouds and rivers. He makes wind, rain and snow. Allah سبحانه وتعالى created this beautiful world for us.

He made the human being to be His *Khalifah,* a vicegerent or deputy, to obey Him. A *Khalifah* is one who must always follow the Commands of His Lord. A *Khalifah* is given power over many things. In doing his duty he must always follow the Commands of Allah سبحانه وتعالى. A *Khalifah* can have command over everything only if he follows the Commands of His Lord.

A Muslim is one who submits his will to Allah سبحانه وتعالى and submits to His commands. Allah سبحانه وتعالى tells us to believe in Him, His Angels, His Books, His Prophets, His *Qadar* (Power to do everything is from Allah سبحانه وتعالى) and in life after death. He wants us to follow His religion Islam, His Book the Qur'ān and His final Messenger, Prophet Muhammad ﷺ.

Allah سبحانه وتعالى knows every thing, sees everything, and hears everything. Nothing happens without His knowledge and permission. There is no other Lord besides Allah سبحانه وتعالى and no higher power than His.

How ever, Allah سبحانه وتعالى is very close to His servants. When we ask for His help, He helps us. When we ask for His guidance, He leads us. We came from Allah سبحانه وتعالى , we belong to Him, and we will return to Him.

WE HAVE LEARNED:

- There is only one God, Allah ﷻ.
- Allah ﷻ has created everything.

DO WE KNOW THESE WORDS?

Angels, deputy, *Khalifah,* prophets, guidance, *'Imān*, vicegerent.

Lesson 4

BELIEF IN ALLAH´S ANGELS

Angels are Allah´s creation. Angels are created to glorify, worship and serve Allah ﷻ. Angels are made of *Nūr,* the Divine Light.

Angels do not eat or drink. They have neither families nor children. They are neither female nor male.

Angels were created long before the creation of Adam ؑ. They have wings two, three and four. No one knows exactly what they look like. They can take different shapes and forms. No one knows the exact number of angels.

Angels praise and glorify Allah ﷻ and serve Him all the time. They do not disobey Him. They always do their duty as they are told. They cannot say, "No" to any work Allah ﷻ wants them to do.

Angels report on us and they will question us in the grave. We do not see Angels but they see us. The Prophets saw the Angels when the Angels brought Allah´s message to them.

Angel Jibril ؑ brought Allah´s *Wahi* (revelation) to the prophets and they saw him. Rasulullah ﷺ saw Angel Jibril many times. Some of his *Sahabah* saw Angel Jibril ؑ when he once came in the form of a human being.

'Izrā'il ؑ, the angel of death, comes to people before their death and takes their souls out of their bodies. He gives the believers the good news of *Jannah.*

Angel Isrāfil ؑ, with the permission of Allah ﷻ, will blow *Aṣ-Ṣūr. Aṣ-Ṣūr* is a special trumpet which has a very loud sound. The noise of *Aṣ-Ṣūr* will wake up the dead people, and gather them in the presence of Allah ﷻ for judgment.

At one point of time, that only Allah ﷻ knows, everything that He has created will come to an end. Only Allah ﷻ will remain. He will bring all of us to life all over again.

Allah ﷻ has made Angel Mikā'il ﷺ to arrange for the rainfall. Two angels named *Munkar* and *Nakīr* will question the dead in the grave. They will ask them about their Religion, their Prophet and their Book.

Two other angels, *Kirāman Kātibīn,* sit on our right and left shoulders. The angel on the right writes whatever good we do. The angel on the left writes whatever bad we do. On the Day of Judgment all our actions will be presented before Allah ﷻ.

WE HAVE LEARNED:

- Allah ﷻ has created angels from the light, called *Nūr*.
- The angels serve Allah ﷻ and glorify Him.
- We cannot see angels but angels can see us.

DO WE KNOW THESE WORDS?

Mikā'il, Munkar, Nakīr, Kiraman Kātibīn, 'Isrāfil, 'Izrā'īl, Aṣ-Ṣūr.

Lesson 5

BELIEF IN THE PROPHETS OF ALLAH سبحانه وتعالى

Allah سبحانه وتعالى has sent many Prophets *('Anbiyā')* and Messengers *(Rusul)* to humankind. A Prophet *(Nabī)* is one whom Allah سبحانه وتعالى has chosen to teach His Message. Allah teaches us through these Prophets about what is coming and what has passed. He tells us the best way to live on earth. He teaches us how to prepare ourselves for the Hereafter.

A Prophet is called *Nabī*. When Allah سبحانه وتعالى chooses a Prophet and prepares him to His cause, He purifies his heart to receive His Message. The Prophet carries the message to his family and his people.

Some Prophets had received Allah's Books. They were asked to carry the Message to all the people around them. They received Allah's Laws to teach people how to live by them. This kind of prophet is called a *Rasūl*, or a Messenger.

Muhmmad ﷺ was a *Nabī* (Prophet) and a *Rasūl* (Messenger). He was *Nabi-Ullah* (the Prophet of Allah) and *Rasūl-Ullah,* (the Messenger of Allah). He is the last Prophet and last Messenger of Allah سبحانه وتعالى. He is "the Seal of the Prophets."

Allah سبحانه وتعالى sent His last and final Message of Islam to humankind through Muhammad ﷺ. Allah سبحانه وتعالى made Muhammad ﷺ the last Prophet.

Allah سبحانه وتعالى has sent Prophets to people all over the world. No one knows the exact number of Prophets that Allah سبحانه وتعالى has sent. The names of twenty-five Prophets are mentioned in the Qur'ān. Every Prophet brought Allah's Message to his people. Every Prophet spoke in the language of his people. All of them taught only one *Dīn* (religion), Islam.

They taught us to:

- Believe in Allah سبحانه وتعالى, our Lord and Creator.
- Believe in Allah's Angels, His Books, His Prophets, and the

Life After Death.

■ Follow Allah's Laws and do not make mischief in the world.

Muslims believe in all the Prophets sent by Allah ﷻ. Prophet Adam ﷺ was the first Prophet of Allah ﷻ. Prophet Muhammad ﷺ is the last and final Prophet and Messenger of Allah ﷻ.

The Prophets were human beings; they were Allah's Servants and Messengers. They were not partners of Allah ﷻ. They were not sons or relative of Allah ﷻ. But they were very special human beings. They were the best of human beings.

The Prophets had firm faith and trust in Allah ﷻ. Their character was noble: they were never selfish or mean. They were truthful, honest and kind. They were obedient to Allah ﷻ and gave His Message to their communities, exactly as they received it.

They were very courageous. When in danger, the Prophets were not afraid. When wrongdoers opposed them, they stood firm. When they were laughed at and tortured, they remained patient. In the Prophets of Allah ﷻ we have the best example of the best human beings.

We Muslims must always follow the teachings of the Qur'ān. We must always follow the *Sunnah* of Rasūlullah ﷺ.

WE HAVE LEARNED:

◈ Muslims believe in all the Prophets of Allah ﷻ.
◈ Prophet Adam ﷺ was the first and Prophet Muhammad ﷺ is the last and final Prophets of Allah ﷻ.
◈ In the Prophets of Allah ﷻ we have the best example to follow.

DO WE KNOW THESE WORDS?

Character, Message, *Nabī*, *Rasūl*, tortured, *Wahi*.

Lesson 6

BELIEF IN THE BOOKS OF ALLAH ﷻ

Allah ﷻ has created us and He loves us. Allah ﷻ has made us His *Khulafā'* (deputies) on earth. Allah ﷻ wants us to believe in Him and worship Him alone. Allah ﷻ wants us to always follow the right path of Islam.

Allah ﷻ sent many Prophets to teach us what Islam is. He chose some of the Prophets and gave them His Books. These Books were Allah's *Wahī* (Revelation). Allah's Books taught people the true *Dīn,* the religion of Islam.

A Prophet who is chosen to receive Allah's *Wahī* is called *Rasūl,* a Messenger. Allah ﷻ gave him His message to deliver to the people. Allah ﷻ sent many Books to people. Most of these Books are lost.

All of these Books have been changed by people through time, except the Qur'ān. Many new ideas have been added to these Books. Some of the teachings of Allah ﷻ have been removed from these Books. It is now very difficult to say what the original message was in those Books.

Allah ﷻ, tells us in the Qur'ān about the following Books:

- The *Ṣuḥuf* (Scriptures) were revealed to Prophet Ibrahim عليه السلام.
- The *Tawrāt* (Torah) was revealed to Prophet Musa عليه السلام.
- The *Zabūr* (Psalms) was revealed to Prophet Dawud عليه السلام.
- The *'Injīl* (Gospels) was revealed to Prophet 'Isa عليه السلام.
- The Qur'ān was revealed to Prophet Muhammad ﷺ.

The *Ṣuḥuf* of Ibrāhīm عليه السلام was lost and nobody knows where it is. Some other books have been lost and only their translations remain. We do not know what their original words were. The Qur'ān is the only Book from Allah ﷻ which has not been changed.

The Qur'ān is the final Revelation of Allah ﷻ. It was revealed in the Arabic language. Allah ﷻ has promised to protect the Qur'ān from any changes. Both the meanings and the words are safeguarded by Allah ﷻ. Allah ﷻ promises in the Qur'ān:

إِنَّا نَحْنُ نَزَّلْنَا ٱلذِّكْرَ وَإِنَّا لَهُۥ لَحَٰفِظُونَ

Indeed! We have revealed the Book, and We shall safeguard it.
(*Al-Hijr* 15:9)

Allah ﷻ has given us the Guidance of the Qur'ān. We must follow its Guidance and practice its teachings. We must learn to read the Qur'ān in Arabic, memorize it, understand its meaning and follow its teachings.

WE HAVE LEARNED:

- Muslims believe in all the revealed Books of Allah ﷻ.
- The five revealed Books of Allah ﷻ are: the *Ṣuḥuf,* the *Zabūr*, the *Tawrāt*, the *'Injīl,* and the Qur'ān.
- The Qur'ān is the final Book of Allah ﷻ.

DO WE KNOW THESE WORDS?

Addition, *'Injīl,* protect, *Ṣuḥuf*, *Tawrāt*, *Zabūr*, guidance.

Lesson 7

AL QADAR: THE POWER OF ALLAH ﷾

Allah ﷾ is our Lord and Creator. He is All-Powerful. He knows everything. He controls everything. Everything happens with His Knowledge. Everything happens by His Permission. Nothing could happen without His Knowledge and Permission. He knows everything that has happened in the past. He knows everything that is happening now. He knows everything that will happen in the future.

He created everything. He created human beings. He gave human beings freedom to act as they please. He gave human beings a will to do what they want.

Allah ﷾ says in the Qur'ān:

وَنَفْسٍ وَمَا سَوَّىٰهَا ﴿٧﴾ فَأَلْهَمَهَا فُجُورَهَا وَتَقْوَىٰهَا ﴿٨﴾
قَدْ أَفْلَحَ مَن زَكَّىٰهَا ﴿٩﴾ وَقَدْ خَابَ مَن دَسَّىٰهَا

And think of the human Spirit and how it is formed and how in it are the powers of doing (both) bad and good. He indeed is successful, who makes it grow in purity. He indeed is unsuccessful, who makes it corrupt.
(*'Ash-Shams* 91:7-10)

Human beings are given a choice by Allah ﷾ to do good or to do evil. By doing good they can earn Allah's Pleasure and *Jannah*. By doing evil they can earn Allah's Anger and *Jahannam*. Those who follow the Guidance of the Qur'ān and the *Sunnah* of Prophet Muhammad ﷺ will be blessed.

People have freedom, but this freedom is given to them by Allah ﷾. They cannot do anything without Allah's Permission. Allah ﷾ has the Knowledge of all the actions that people do. This is called *Qadar,* the Power of Allah ﷾ of knowing everything, recording it and permitting it to happen.

Allah ﷾ has given us the power to choose between right and wrong as well as the minds to make our own decisions. We are, therefore, responsible for all of our actions. We will be judged for our actions on the Day of Judgment. Our freedom is special; it is a gift from Allah سبحانه وتعالى. We must use it properly. However, Allah's freedom is complete. He can use it as He wishes.

This Power of Allah سبحانه وتعالى to do everything He wants, knowing everything that will happen and permitting it to happen, is called the *Qadar*.

WE HAVE LEARNED:

- Allah سبحانه وتعالى has Knowledge of everything and Power over everything.
- Allah سبحانه وتعالى has given us freedom to choose between good and bad.
- Allah سبحانه وتعالى has Knowledge of our actions and has got them recorded.

DO WE KNOW THESE WORDS?

Complete, inspired, *Qadar,* Record, purity, spirit.

Lesson 8

LIFE AFTER DEATH

One day Allah سبحانه وتعالى will bring an end to this world, and whatever is in it. This day is called the Last Day or *'Al-Qiyāmah,* the Day of Judgment. We are now living in *'Ad-Dunyā,* the world. We shall rise after death in a new world. That world is called *'Al-'Akhirah,* the Hereafter.

Only Allah سبحانه وتعالى is Eternal. Eternal means living forever. Allah has always been alive and He will never die.

We live in this world for a fixed time. Our life and death in this world are a test from Allah سبحانه وتعالى.

The Qur'ān says:

ٱلَّذِى خَلَقَ ٱلْمَوْتَ وَٱلْحَيَوٰةَ لِيَبْلُوَكُمْ أَيُّكُمْ أَحْسَنُ عَمَلًا ۚ وَهُوَ ٱلْعَزِيزُ ٱلْغَفُورُ

(He is Allah) Who created Death and Life that He may see who is best in deeds.
(*'Al-Mulk* 67:2)

Allah سبحانه وتعالى has fixed the time of life and death for everyone. No one knows the time of his or her death. Only Allah سبحانه وتعالى knows. No one can tell how his or her death will occur. It comes to young people and old people alike.

The Qur'ān informs us:

لِكُلِّ أُمَّةٍ أَجَلٌ ۚ إِذَا جَآءَ أَجَلُهُمْ فَلَا يَسْتَـْٔخِرُونَ سَاعَةً ۖ وَلَا يَسْتَقْدِمُونَ

For every people there is a fixed time; when their time comes, they shall not remain behind for an hour, nor can they go before their time
(*Yūnus* 10:49)

When we are laid to rest in the grave, the two angels *Munkar* and *Nakīr* will ask us three questions. *In-shā'-Allah,* we will be able to answer them correctly:

1. Who is your *Rabb?*
   "My *Rabb* (Lord) is Allah", we should reply.
2. What is your *Dīn?*
   "My *Dīn* (religion) is Islam", we should respond.
3. Who is your Prophet?
   "My Prophet is Muhammad," we should answer.

We will then be laid to sleep and will wake up on the Day of Judgment. Non-believers will not be able to answer these questions. They will remain in punishment until the Day of Judgment. Allah ﷾ will safeguard our souls and unite them with our new bodies on the Day of Judgment.

All the dead would rise from their graves and their new lives will begin. Everyone will be judged for their deeds.

The Qur'ān informs us:

فَمَن يَعْمَلْ مِثْقَالَ ذَرَّةٍ خَيْرًا يَرَهُۥ ۝٧
وَمَن يَعْمَلْ مِثْقَالَ ذَرَّةٍ شَرًّا يَرَهُۥ ۝٨

Whoever does good (even) equal to an atom's weight, shall see it.
Whoever does evil (even) equal to an atom's weight, shall see it.
(*'Az-Zalzalah* 99:7-8)

Those who enter *Jannah* will be there forever; those who enter *Jahannam* will need Allah's Mercy to get out.

WE HAVE LEARNED:

- Everything that is created will come to an end on the Day of *'Al-Qiyāmah.*
- Only Allah ﷾ is Eternal.
- Allah ﷾ will recreate everyone and judge them for their deeds.

DO WE KNOW THESE WORDS?

Eternal, the Last Day, *'Al-Qiyāmah,* Soul.

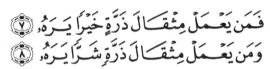

Lesson 9

THE LAST DAY

All those who are born will die one day. On that day everything created by Allah ﷾ will come to an end. Every human being who has died will be raised one day. That day is called the Day of *Qiyāmah,* the Day of Judgment. That day is also called the Last Day. It will not be like any other day. It will be a very long day, consisting of hundreds of years.

On the Last Day Allah ﷾ will ask Angel *'Isrāfīl* to blow *'Aṣ-Ṣūr,* the Trumpet. Everything will start crumbling, falling, crushing and breaking.

On that day the mountains will fly like cotton and dust. The whole world will collapse and will come to an end. Only Allah ﷾ will remain.

On that Day Allah ﷾ will ask:

لِّمَنِ ٱلْمُلْكُ ٱلْيَوْمَ ۖ لِلَّهِ ٱلْوَٰحِدِ ٱلْقَهَّارِ

Whose will be all the Power that day? It will belong only to Allah, the One, the Most Powerful.
(*Ghāfir* 40:16)

There will be no one on that day to answer Allah ﷾. Then Allah ﷾ will recreate the whole world. Everyone will come back to life. The people will rise from their graves. The Day of Judgment will then begin.

Everyone will be presented before Allah ﷾. The books of those who believed and did good deeds will be in their right hands. The books of those who did not believe and did bad deeds will be in their left hands.

Everyone's actions will then be weighed. Only Allah ﷾ will decide who will go to *Jannah* or *Jahannam.* Allah ﷾ is a Fair Judge and Kind Lord. No one will be able to help anyone else. No one will be able to speak for anyone else. Everyone will be responsible for his or her own actions.

Only Rasūlullāh ﷺ will be permitted to make *Shafā'ah* for his *'Ummah*. *Shafā'ah* means to ask Allah ﷻ for forgiveness and mercy. Allah ﷻ will save many people through His Mercy and through the *Shafā'ah* of Rasūlullāh ﷺ.

Then people will be made to walk over the bridge of *Aṣ-Ṣirāt*. The bridge of *Aṣ-Ṣirāt* is thin and sharp. The bridge of *Aṣ-Ṣirāt* is built over the Fire of Hell. The Believers will pass over the bridge like a breeze.

Prophet Muhammad ﷺ will meet his *'Ummah* on the banks of the river *'Al-Kawthar*. *'Al-Kawthar* is a special Gift of Allah ﷻ to Rasullullah ﷺ for his *'Ummah*. It's water is whiter than milk and sweeter than honey. Those who will drink the water of *'Al-Kawthar* will never be thirsty again. We all pray that Allah ﷻ be kind to us on the Last Day and bless us with the *Shafā'ah* of Rasūlullāh ﷺ.

WE HAVE LEARNED:

- People will be judged for their actions on the Day of Judgment.
- The *Shafā'ah* of Rasulullah ﷺ and the Mercy of Allah ﷻ will help many people.
- The happiness of *Jannah* and punishment of *Jahannam* are forever.

DO WE KNOW THESE WORDS?

'Al-Kawthar, 'Isrāfīl, Shafā'ah, Aṣ-Ṣirāt, 'Aṣ-Ṣūr

Lesson 10

ACTS OF A MUSLIM

We have learned about the beliefs of a Muslim. Now, we know that every Muslims believes that:

- Allah ﷻ is the Creator and Allah ﷻ is One.
- Allah ﷻ has sent His Messengers to teach mankind His Religion, Islam.
- Allah ﷻ has given His Books to some of the Prophets.
- Allah ﷻ has created Angels as His Servants.
- Allah ﷻ has the Power to know everything, record everything and permit it to happen; this Power of Allah is called *Qadar*.
- There is another life after death and we will return to Allah ﷻ.

Those who have these beliefs are called Muslims.

A Muslim is required to do certain things for the sake of Allah ﷻ. Leading one's life according to the Commands of Allah ﷻ is an act of *'Ibādah. 'Ibādah* means to worship Allah ﷻ and to obey His commands. The entire life of a Muslim, if led according to the teachings of Islam, is *'Ibādah.*

The *Sunnah* of Rasūlullāh ﷺ shows us how to lead an Islamic life. A Muslim is required by Allah ﷻ to live and act in a special way. Every Muslim should:

- Say the *Shahādah* with his or her tongue and believe it in the heart.
- Pray five times a day.
- Give *Zakāt,* a part of his savings to the poor and needy.
- Keep the fast *(Ṣawm)* in the month of *Ramaḍān.*
- Go to the city of Makkah for *Ḥajj* once in his or her life time if he or she can afford it.

These are five acts of *'Ibādah,* a Muslim is required to do to please Allah ﷻ.

These acts of *'Ibādah* are also called the five *Arkān,* the pillars of Islam. Pillars are the support that help a building stand. The five pillars of Islam support the faith of a Muslim and help him or her stand up against *Shaiṭān.* As a building cannot stand without the support of the pillars, the faith of a Muslim cannot stand without the support of the five *'Arkān.*

We have learned about the *Shahādah* in an earlier lesson; let us learn about the other pillars now. Let us read the following lessons and learn about the other four *'Arkān* of Islam. Let us learn to practice the five *'Arkān* of Islam.

WE HAVE LEARNED:

- Every Muslim must believe in *Tawḥīd,* the Prophets of Allah ﷻ, the Books of Allah ﷻ, the Angels, the *Qadar* and Life After Death.
- Every Muslim has to perform five acts of *'Ibādah*, which are: the *Shahādah, Ṣalāh, Ṣawm, Zakāh,* and *Ḥajj.*
- These five acts of *'Ibādah* are called five *'Arkān ul-'Islām,* the Five Pillars of Islam.

DO WE KNOW THESE WORDS?

'Arkān, Farḍ, Farā'id, 'Ibādah, pillar, worship.

Lesson 11

WHY DO WE PRAY?

Offering the five daily prayers is an obligation, or *Farḍ,* on every Muslim. It is the obligation of every adult Muslim to offer five daily prayers. Allah ﷻ says in the Qur'ān:

إِنَّ ٱلصَّلَوٰةَ كَانَتْ عَلَى ٱلْمُؤْمِنِينَ كِتَٰبًا مَّوْقُوتًا

Ṣalāh is made obligatory for the Believers to be offered at fixed times
(*An-Nisā'* 4:103)

The main purpose of our life is to worship Allah ﷻ and obey His commands. *Ṣalāh* is the best form of worship and obedience to Allah ﷻ. Allah ﷻ says in the Qur'ān:

وَمَا خَلَقْتُ ٱلْجِنَّ وَٱلْإِنسَ إِلَّا لِيَعْبُدُونِ

I have created the *Jinn* and humans for no other purpose except to worship Me.
(*Adh-Dhāriyāt* 51:56)

Allah ﷻ has reminded us in the Qur'ān repeatedly to establish the *Ṣalāh.* This means there is no real Islamic life without establishing the *Ṣalāh.* When we offer *Ṣalāh* in a *Masjid* with *Jamā'ah* we come closer to each other. We get to know each other better. Then it is easier to plan to work together for Islam and our society.

Islam establishes our relations with Allah ﷻ directly. The *Ṣalāh* is the best method of establishing our direct relationship with Allah ﷻ. In offering *Ṣalāh* we stand five times a day face to face with Allah ﷻ. We pray to Him directly and He answers our prayers:

وَقَالَ رَبُّكُمُ ٱدْعُونِىٓ أَسْتَجِبْ لَكُمْ

And your Lord says: Call on me,I will answer to you
(*Ghāfir* 40:60)

Offering *Ṣalāh* creates the habit of discipline and regularity in us. Then our lives become a way of worshipping Allah ﷻ.

The *Ṣalāh* makes us lead a pure and clean life. Being in the company of believers makes us do the right things. It is said, "One is known by the company he keeps". Allah ﷻ says in the Qur'ān:

يَٰٓأَيُّهَا ٱلَّذِينَ ءَامَنُوا۟ ٱتَّقُوا۟ ٱللَّهَ وَكُونُوا۟ مَعَ ٱلصَّٰدِقِينَ

O you who believe! Be conscious of Allah and be in the company of the truthful.

(*ʹAt-Tawbah* 9:119)

Thinking of Allah ﷻ makes our hearts pure of any wrongdoing. Thinking of Allah ﷻ also makes our intentions pure. Our life becomes a good example for others to follow. The Qur'ān tells us:

وَأَقِمِ ٱلصَّلَوٰةَ ۖ إِنَّ ٱلصَّلَوٰةَ تَنْهَىٰ عَنِ ٱلْفَحْشَآءِ وَٱلْمُنكَرِ ۗ

And establish *Salah,* for indeed *Ṣalāh* forbids one from indecent and evil acts.

(*ʹAl-ʹAnkabut* 29:45)

The most important thing about *Ṣalāh* is that we offer it to show our love and obedience of Allah ﷻ.

WE HAVE LEARNED:

- *Ṣalāh* is an obligation for every adult Muslim.
- *Ṣalāh* makes us do good and avoid evil.
- We show our love and obedience to Allah ﷻ through *Ṣalāh*.

DO WE KNOW THESE WORDS?

Command, Discipline, Establish, Obedience, Regularity.

Lesson 12

PREPARATION FOR THE *ṢALĀH*

Islam teaches us cleanliness and purity in both body and heart. The Arabic Islamic word for cleanliness and purity is *Ṭahārah*. *Ṭahārah* means both, cleanliness of the body and purity of the heart.

Cleanliness does not always mean *Ṭahārah*. We shall understand the meaning of *Ṭahārah* more clearly after this lesson. A clean and pure person and place is called *Ṭāhir*.

The *Qur'ān* teaches us:

إِنَّ ٱللَّهَ يُحِبُّ ٱلتَّوَّٰبِينَ وَيُحِبُّ ٱلْمُتَطَهِّرِينَ

Surely, Allah loves those who ask for His Forgiveness
and He loves those who are pure and clean.
(*'Al-Baqarah* 2:222)

Rasūlullāh ﷺ taught us:

الطَّهَارَةُ شَطْرُ الإِيمَانِ.

"*Ṭahārah* is half of one's faith".

Allah ﷻ wants us to offer *Ṣalāh* when we are pure in our spirit and in body. The *Ṣalāh* is one of the ways to clean our hearts. If our hearts are pure and our intentions are right, Allah ﷻ accepts our prayers.

The *Ṭahārah* is an essential part of *Ṣalāh*. If there is no *Ṭahārah*, *Ṣalāh* is not accepted by Allah ﷻ. First of all, the place where we stand for *Ṣalāh* must be clean. Most Muslims use clean *Sajjadah* (prayer rug) for the *Ṣalāh*. The clothes we wear for *Ṣalāh* must also be *Ṭāhir*, pure and clean. Our bodies must also be *Ṭāhir*.

When we offer *Ṣalāh*, our bodies, clothes and place of prayer must be clean from any *Najāsah*. *Najāsah* is the opposite of *Ṭahārah*. *Najāssah* is impurity and uncleaness, whether one sees it or not. Some of the examples of *Najāsah* are:

- Urine
- Excrements
- Blood
- Pus
- All products from unclean things like pig, liquor etc.

There are conditions when we must take a bath to have *Ṭahārah*. We shall discuss those conditions in the next book at junior level. We must make *Wuḍū'* before we offer *Ṣalāh*.

WE HAVE LEARNED:

- Allah ﷻ loves those people who are *Ṭāhir*, pure and clean.
- *Ṭahārah* is an essential condition for the *Ṣalāh*.
- *Najāsah* is the opposite of *Ṭahārah* and must be cleaned.

DO WE KNOW THESE WORDS?

Essential, *Najāsah, Ṭahārah, Ṭāhir.*

Lesson 13

MAKING *WUḌŪ'*

We must have *Wuḍū'* before we offer *Ṣalāh*. *Wuḍū'* means purity and cleanliness. *Wuḍū'* should be made with clean and pure water. In making *Wuḍū'*, we wash certain parts of the body. Most of the parts must be washed three times.

Rasūlullāh ﷺ showed us how to make *Wuḍū'*. We should make *Wuḍū'* in the same way as he did. There are certain steps in making *Wuḍū'*. We shall go over each step one by one.

First of all, we should declare the intention of making *Wuḍū'*. We may say the intention in Arabic or in our own language.

نَوَيْتُ أَنْ أَتَوَضَّأَ لِلصَّلاَةِ

I have the intention to make *Wuḍū'* for the *Ṣalāh*.

Remember, we wash certain parts of the body three times, except making the *Masḥ*.
Say *Bismillāh ir-Raḥmān ir-Raḥīm,* and start making *Wuḍū'* now:

1. We should **wash our hands** three times up to the wrists.

2. We should **rinse the mouth** with water three times.

3. We should **sniff water in the nostrils** three times to wash them clean.

4. We should **wash our face** three times:
   a) from the forehead to the chin;
   b) and from ear to ear.

WUḌU'

Wash Hands
(Three times)

Rinse Mouth
(Three times)

Sniff Water in the Nostrils
(Three times)

Wash face from Forehead to Chin
(Three times)

WUḌU'

Wash Face from
Ear to Ear

Wash Arms Up to the Elbow
(Three times)

Do *Masḥ* of the Head
Starting from the Forehead

Masḥ-Wipe Head from
Forehead to Back of Neck

Masḥ-
Clean Ears
With
"Shahadah"
Finger

Masḥ-
Wipe Back
of Neck
With Back
of Hands

Wash Feet
up to the
ankles
Right foot
first

5. We should wash the arms up to the elbow three times, first right arm and then left.
6. We should do *Masḥ* of the head only one time and there are five steps to it:

   A. We must first wet our hands with water, wipe our head starting from the forehead and over to the back of the neck.
   B. Clean the ears with wet *Shahādah* (index) finger.
   C. Pass wet thumbs behind the ears, bringing them from the top of ears to the lobe.
   D. Wipe the right arm up to the elbow with left hand and then the left arm with the right hand.

7. We should wash our feet (right foot first) up to the ankles.

If we put on socks made of leather or strong and thick material after making *Wuḍū* we can make *Masḥ* on them for the next twenty four hours, instead of completely washing the feet while performing the *Wuḍū*. Remember, some *'Ulamā'* (teachers of Islam) permit *Masḥ* only on the leather socks. Ask your parents and teachers what do they prefer. When making *Masḥ*, wet your hands and wipe the upper parts of your socks gently starting from the toe.

It is *Sunnah* to say *Shahādah* at the completion of the *Wuḍū*. If you are making *Wuḍū* in a bathroom which has a toilet, don't say *Shahādah* then. Wait till you come out and then say it.

It is better if you close the cover of the toilet before starting the *Wuḍū*. Make Sure to leave the bathroom or the place of the *Wuḍū* dry and clean.

Shahādah and *Du'ā* after *Wuḍū*

أَشْهَدُ أَنْ لاَ إِلَهَ إِلاَّ اللهُ ، وَحْدَهُ لاَ شَرِيكَ لَهُ ،
وَأَشْهَدُ أَنَّ مُحَمَّدًا عَبْدُهُ وَرَسُولُهُ .
اَللَّهُمَّ اجْعَلْنِي مِنَ التَّوَّابِينَ ، واجْعَلْنِي مِنَ الْمُتَطَهِّرِينَ .
سُبْحَانَكَ اللَّهُمَّ وَبِحَمْدِكَ ، أَشْهَدُ أَنْ لاَ إِلَهَ إِلاَّ أَنْتَ ، أَسْتَغْفِرُكَ وَأَتُوبُ إِلَيْكَ .

'Ashhadu 'an-lā llāha ill-Allāhu wahdahu lā sharikā lahu wa ashhadu anna Muhammadan 'abduhu wa Rasūlullāh, Allahumma-j 'alni minat tawwabina wa-j 'alni minal mutatahhirin. Subhanaka-llahumma wa bihamdika. Ashhadu an la ilaha illa 'anta, 'Astaghfiruka wa-'atubu ilaika.

I bear witness that there is no god but Allah Who is alone without partner and I bear witness that Muhammad is His servant and His Prophet. O Allah, make me one of those who turn in repentance, and make me one of those who purify themselves. Glory is to You, O Allah, and Yours is the praise. I bear witness that there is no god but You. I seek Your forgiveness, and I turn to You in repentance.

WE HAVE LEARNED:

- *Wuḍū* is required before the *Ṣalāh.*
- *Wuḍū* is done in a specific way.
- We must leave the place of *Wuḍū* tidy and dry.

DO WE KNOW THESE WORDS?

Intention, nostrils, *Masḥ*, rinse, specific

FURTHER HELP:

Teachers will find it helpful to have IQRA' CHART OF THE *ṢALAH* AND *WUḌU* in the classroom and explain the steps of *Wuḍū* and *Ṣalāh* with its help. Color the steps of *Wuḍū* in COLORING BOOK OF *ṢALAH*.

Lesson 14

TAYAMMUM

In case we are not able to make *Wuḍū*, Allah ﷻ permits us to make *Tayammum*. *Tayammum* is dry cleaning without the use of water. Allah ﷻ wants to make things easy for us. Allah ﷻ says in the Qur'an:

يُرِيدُ ٱللَّهُ بِكُمُ ٱلْيُسْرَ وَلَا يُرِيدُ بِكُمُ ٱلْعُسْرَ

Allah wants to make things easy for you.
He does not want to make things difficult for you.
(*'Al-Baqarah* 2:185)

The following may be reasons for not being able to make *Wuḍū*:

- The time for *Ṣalāh* may be coming to an end and there may be no water available.
- One is too sick to make *Wuḍū*.
- The water available is too little and it is necessary to save it for drinking.

The steps for *Tayammum* are the following:

1. Make the *Niyyah* of *Tayammum*.
2. Start by saying, *Bismillāh ir-Raḥmān ir-Raḥīm*.
3. Rub both your hands lightly on clean earth, dust or some dusty place (wall, wood etc.).
4. Blow the dust from your hands.
5. Wipe your entire face from forehead to chin with your hands.
6. Wipe again, both of your hands on the earth, dust, or dusty object once more.
7. Wipe the right arm, from elbow to wrist, with the left hand.
8. Wipe the left arm, from elbow to wrist, with the right hand.

Tayammum

Rub or Put Both Hands on Clean Earth or Dust

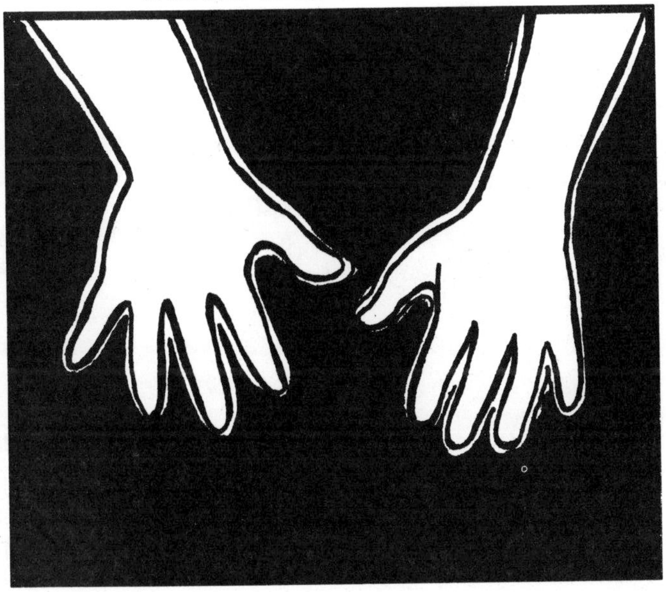

Blow Dust from Hands

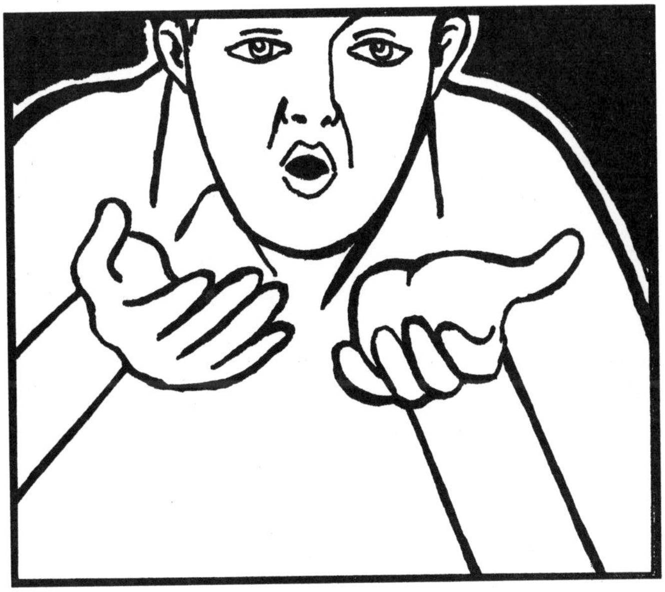

Wipe Entire Face from Forehead to Chin

wipe arms from Elbow to Wrist

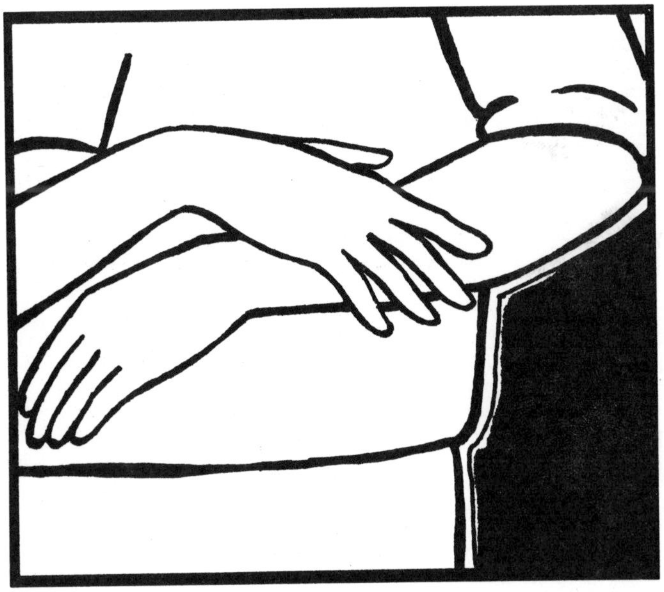

The *Tayammum* comes to an end when the reasons for making it come to an end, that is:

- When water becomes available.
- When a person recovers from sickness.

Wuḍū and *Tayammum* both come to an end when:

- There is a discharge of gas, urine and stool, etc. from private parts.
- There is flow of blood or pus from any part of the body.
- Vomiting (a mouthful) takes place.
- One falls asleep.

Tayammum must be repeated before each *Ṣalāh*. Whereas, *Wuḍū*, if maintained, need not be repeated before every *Ṣalāh*.

WE HAVE LEARNED:

- Allah ﷻ wants to make things easy for us.
- We can make *Tayammum* when making *Wuḍū* is not possible.
- We must make a fresh *Tayammum* before we make *Ṣalāh*.

DO WE KNOW THESE WORDS?

Condition, discharge, mouthful, *Niyyah,* recover, *Tayammum.*

Lesson 15

MAKING THE *'ADHĀN*

Every religion has its own way of calling people to prayers. The Islamic way of calling people to *Ṣalāh* is the *'Adhān*. By calling the *'Adhān* we praise Allah ﷻ and invite people to Allah's way.

Rasulullah ﷺ decided in favor of the *'Adhān* on the advice of his two *Ṣaḥābah*, Abdullah ibn Zaid ؓ and Umar ibn ul-Khattab ؓ. They both had dreams about the *'Adhān*.

'Adhān means to call or to declare. The person who makes the *'Adhān* is called the *Mu'adhdhin*. There is a great reward for calling the *'Adhān*. Allah ﷻ says in the Qur'ān:

وَمَنْ أَحْسَنُ قَوْلًا مِّمَّن دَعَآ إِلَى ٱللَّهِ وَعَمِلَ صَٰلِحًا وَقَالَ إِنَّنِى مِنَ ٱلْمُسْلِمِينَ

Who is better in speech than the one who calls people to Allah, does good and says, "Indeed, I am one of those who are Muslims".
(*Fuṣṣilat* 41:33)

A *Mu'adhdhin* calls people to come and offer *Ṣalāh* in *Jamā'ah*. It is preferred if the *Mu'adhdhin* also says the *'Iqāmah*.

A *Mu'adhdhin* should be a person whose voice is loud and clear. The first *Mu'adhdhin* of Rasūlullāh ﷺ was Bilal ibn Rabah ؓ. Bilal ؓ was an African slave who was freed by Abu Bakr ؓ, when Abu Bakr ؓ paid the money to Bilal's owner. Bilal ؓ was one of the first Muslims and a *Ṣaḥābī* of Rasūlullāh ﷺ.

The *'Adhān* is called from a place where it can be heard by a large number of people. Many *Masājid* have tall minarets for calling the *'Adhān*. Now many *Masājid* in Muslim countries use loud speakers to call the *'Adhān*. In the United States and Canada, the *'Adhān* is usually called by the *Mu'adhdhin* inside the *Masjid*.

Some people now use *'Adhān* clocks to remind them of the time for *Ṣalāh*. Many Islamic centers publish charts of the times of *Ṣalāh*. When we hear the *'Adhān*, we should go to a *Masjid* in the neighborhood. If we are not living close to a *Masjid* we should say the *'Adhān* on regular time at home.

We must try to offer *Ṣalāh* in *Jamā'ah*. The reward for the *Ṣalāh* of *Jama'ah* is twenty-seven times more than the *Ṣalāh* offered alone!

WE HAVE LEARNED:

- The *'Adhān* is the Islamic way to call people to prayer.
- The person who calls the *'Adhān* is called a *Mu'adhdhin*.
- It is best to call the *'Adhān* on time and offer *Ṣalāh* in *Jamā'ah*.

DO WE KNOW THESE WORDS?

Invite, Praise, Preferred, *Jamā'ah*, *Mu'adhdhin*,

THE STORY OF THE *'ADHĀN*

In Makkah the number of Muslims was small. They could make *Jamā'ah* without any call. When Rasūlullāh ﷺ arrived in Madīnah, the number of Muslims started to increase.

Rasūlullāh ﷺ built *Masjid un-Nabi* to offer *Ṣalāh* regularly. By the second year of the *Hijrah,* the number of Muslims had increased. The people announced in a loud voice, *"Aṣ-Ṣalāt ul-Jamā'ah*, the *Ṣalāh* for *Jamā'ah* is ready." Those who heard this call came to join the *Ṣalāh*. Muslims felt the need for a better way to inform people to come to *Ṣalāh*. Rasūlullāh ﷺ asked his *Ṣaḥābah* for their advice.

Some *Ṣaḥābah* suggested that Muslims, like the Jews, should blow a horn to announce the time for the *Ṣalāh*. Others said, the Muslims might ring bells like the Christians do in their Churches. A few proposed that the Muslims, like the fire-worshippers, kindle a fire to call people to pray. Rasūlullāh ﷺ was not satisfied with any of these ideas. He waited to hear a better idea or to receive guidance from Allah ﷻ.

One day, a *Ṣaḥābī* named Abdullah ibn Zaid ؓ, came to Rasūlullāh ﷺ and said, "O Messenger of Allah! I had a beautiful dream last night".

"What was the dream you saw?" Rasūlullāh ﷺ asked Zaid ؓ.

Abdullah ibn Zaid ؓ answered, "I have seen that a man wearing garments taught me the words of the *'Adhān* and advised me to call people to prayer with these words". He then recited the words for the *'Adhān.*

The words were beautiful and full of meaning. Rasūlullāh ﷺ recognized that the dream of Abdullah ibn Zaid ؓ was true. He asked Abdullah ؓ to teach the words of *'Adhān* to Bilal ؓ. Bilal ؓ, a *Ṣaḥābi* of Rasūlullāh ﷺ was a freed Abyssinian slave; he had a loud and beautiful voice.

Bilal ؓ stood up and called the *'Adhān*. The voice of Bilal ؓ resounded throughout Madinah. People came running to *Masjid un-Nabi.* Umar ؓ was one of the persons who came and said, "O Messenger of Allah an angel taught me the same words in my dream last night."

Rasūlullāh ﷺ accepted this *'Adhān* as the official call to the *Ṣalāh*. Bilal ؓ became the first *Mu'adhdhin* of Islam.

Lesson 16

LEARNING TO MAKE THE *'ADHĀN*

The *'Adhān* must be called for each *Ṣalāh* to invite people to prayer. It is a *Sunnah* to hear the *'Adhān* and to respond to the *'Adhān*. The *Mu'adhdhin* stands up facing the *Qiblah,* places his index fingers in his ears and calls the *'Adhān*.

When we hear the *'Adhān* we must stop talking. We should listen to the *'Adhān* and answer it. The following is the *'Adhān* and its response:

THE *'ADHĀN*

1. اَللّٰهُ أَكْبَرُ ، اَللّٰهُ أَكْبَرُ

'Allāhu 'Akbar, 'Allāhu 'Akbar
'Allāhu 'Akbar, 'Allāhu 'Akbar
Allah is the Greatest!

2. أَشْهَدُ أَنْ لاَ إِلَهَ إِلاَّ اَللّٰهُ

'Ashhadu 'an-lā llāha ill-Allāh
'Ashhadu 'an-lā llāha ill-Allāh
I bear witness that there is no god but Allah

3. أَشْهَدُ أَنَّ مُحَمَّدًا رَسُولُ اللّٰهِ

'Ashhadu 'anna Muhammadar Rasūlullāh
'Ashhadu 'anna Muhammadar Rasūlullāh
I bear witness that Muhammad is the Messenger of Allah

THE RESPONSE

اَللّٰهُ أَكْبَرُ ، اللهُ أَكْبَرُ

'Allāhu 'Akbar, 'Allāhu 'Akbar
'Allāhu 'Akbar, 'Allāhu 'Akbar
Allah is the Greatest!

أَشْهَدُ أَنْ لاَ إِلَهَ إِلاَّ اَللّٰهُ

'Ashhadu 'an-lā llāha ill-Allāh
'Ashhadu 'an-lā llāha ill-Allāh
I bear witness that there is no god but Allah

أَشْهَدُ أَنَّ مُحَمَّدًا رَسُولُ اللّٰهِ

'Ashhadu 'anna Muhammadar Rasūlullāh
'Ashhadu 'anna Muhammadar Rasūlullāh
I bear witness that Muhammad is the Messenger of Allah

4. حَيَّ عَلَى الصَّلاَةِ

Ḥayya 'ala-ṣ-Ṣalāh
Ḥayya 'ala-ṣ-Ṣalāh
Come to the *Ṣalāh*.

لاَ حَوْلَ وَلاَ قُوَّةَ إِلاَّ بِاللَّهِ

La ḥawla wa lā quwwata 'illa billāh
La ḥawla wa lā quwwata 'illa billāh
There is no force and no power
except the Power of Allah

5. حَيَّ عَلَى الْفَلاحِ

Ḥayya 'ala-al-falāḥ
Ḥayya 'ala-al-falāḥ
Come to the Success.

لاَ حَوْلَ وَلاَ قُوَّةَ إِلاَّ بِاللَّهِ

La ḥawla wa lā quwwata 'illa billāh
La ḥawla wa lā quwwata 'illa billāh
There is no force and no power
except the Power of Allah.

6. اللَّهُ أَكْبَرُ ، اللَّهُ أَكْبَرُ

'Allāhu 'Akbar, 'Allāhu 'Akbar
Allah is the Greatest!

اَللَّهُ أَكْبَرُ ، اللَّهُ أَكْبَرُ

'Allāhu 'Akbar, 'Allāhu 'Akbar
Allah is the Greatest!

7. لاَ إِلَهَ إِلاَّ اللَّهُ

Lā llāha ill-Allāh
There is no god but Allah.

لاَ إِلَهَ إِلاَّ اللَّهُ

Lā llāha ill-Allāh
There is no god but Allah.

In the *Ṣalāh* of *'al-Fajr,* after *"ḥayya 'alal-falāh"*, we add the following:

اَلصَّلاةُ خَيْرٌ مِنَ النَّوْمِ

'Aṣ-Ṣalātu Khair-um-min-an-nawm
'Aṣ-Ṣalātu Khair-um-min-an-nawm
Prayer is better than sleep

اَلصَّلاةُ خَيْرٌ مِنَ النَّوْمِ

'Aṣ-Ṣalātu Khair-um-min-an-nawm
'Aṣ-Ṣalātu Khair-um-min-an-nawm
Prayer is better than sleep

Ṣalāh is a gift of Allah ﷻ to Muslims through Prophet Muhammad ﷺ. Muslims invoke Allah's Blessings on Rasūlullāh ﷺ as the *'Adhān* ends by saying:

اَللَّهُمَّ رَبَّ هَذِهِ الدَّعْوَةِ التَّامَّةِ ، وَالصَّلاَةِ الْقَائِمَةِ ،
آتِ مُحَمَّدًا الْوَسِيلَةَ وَالْفَضِيلَةَ ، وَالدَّرَجَةَ الرَّفِيعَةَ ،
وَابْعَثْهُ الْمَقَامَ الْمَحْمُودَ الَّذِي وَعَدْتَهُ ،
وَارْزُقْنَا شَفَاعَتَهُ يَوْمَ الْقِيَامَةِ ، إِنَّكَ لاَ تُخْلِفُ الْمِيعَادَ .

'Allahumma Rabba hādhihi-d-da' wati-t-tāmmati wa ṣ-Ṣalāt il-qā'imati 'ati Muḥammada nil-wasilata wal-faḍilata, wa-d-darajata r-rafi'ah wab'ath-hu al-maqāma al-Maḥmūda-al-ladhī wa'adta-hu warzuqnā shafā'atahu, yawmāl Qiyāmah, 'inna-ka la tukhlif ul-mī'ād

O Allah! Lord of this perfect call and the establishing of *Ṣalāh*, bless Muhammad with the intercession and the excellent position, and admit him to the praiseworthy position You have promised him, and favor us with his *Shafa'ah* (Intercession), Indeed You never break Your promises.

After an interval of a short time, the *'Iqamah* is called by the *Mu'adhdhin*. The *'Iqamah* invites everyone to stand up for *Ṣalāh*.

In *'Iqamah* we use the words of the *'Adhān*, but after *"Ḥayya 'alā-l-falāḥ"*, we add the following words:

قَدْ قَامَتِ الصَّلاَةُ	قَدْ قَامَتِ الصَّلاَةُ
Qād qāmat iṣ-Ṣalāh	*Qād qāmat iṣ-Ṣalāh*
The *Ṣalāh* is ready	The *Ṣalāh* is ready

When we hear the words of *Qād qāmat iṣ-Ṣalāh,* we all must stand up for *Ṣalāh* . We must stand in straight rows, shoulder to shoulder, facing the *Qiblah* and behind the *'Imām.*

WE HAVE LEARNED:

- The *'Adhān* must be called before each *Ṣalāh* in a *Masjid.*
- The *Iqāmah* is called to invite people to stand up for *Ṣalāh*.
- We respond to the *'Adhān* and say *Du'ā* after the *'Adhān.*

DO WE KNOW THESE WORDS?

Intercession, *'Iqāmah,* praiseworthy, *Qiblah, Shafā'ah.*

Lesson 17

CONDITIONS FOR THE *ṢALAH*

Allah ﷻ has told us to offer *Ṣalāh* five times a day. We should not miss any prayer. Allah ﷻ promises in the Qur'ān:

وَالَّذِينَ هُمْ عَلَىٰ صَلَاتِهِمْ يُحَافِظُونَ ﴿٣٤﴾ أُولَٰئِكَ فِي جَنَّاتٍ مُكْرَمُونَ

And those who guard their *Ṣalāh*: such will be the honored ones in the *Jannah* full of blessings.
(*'Al-Ma'ārij* 70:34-35)

The time of *Ṣalāh* has been fixed by Allah ﷻ and it must always be said on time. Allah ﷻ promises *Jannah* to:

الَّذِينَ هُمْ عَلَىٰ صَلَاتِهِمْ دَائِمُونَ

...Those who are regular in offering their *Ṣalāh*.
(*'Al-Ma'ārij* 70:23)

Allah ﷻ told us the times for each *Ṣalāh*. When the prayer time comes, we should not be late in offering *Ṣalāh*. Rasulullah ﷺ said that his most favorite thing was to offer *Ṣalāh* on time.

We should offer *Ṣalāh* in peace. We should turn off the radio and television. We should ask everyone to be quiet, and be quiet ourselves.

When making *Ṣalāh* we should feel as if we are standing in front of Allah ﷻ and are looking at Him. We should know that Allah ﷻ is surely watching us. We are offering *Ṣalāh* for Allah ﷻ and we should feel that He is present. We make *Sunnah Ṣalāh* individually and *Fard Ṣalāh* with the *Jama'ah* behind an *'Imām*.

Jamā'ah means a group of people together. We should offer *Ṣalāh* in *Jamā'ah* with other Muslims in a *Masjid*. If there is no *Masjid* in our neighborhood, we must offer *Jamā'ah* with our family members at home. The reward of offering *Ṣalāh* with *Jamā'ah* is twenty-seven times more than of offering it alone.

We should line up for *Ṣalāh* in *Jamā'ah*. We should stand in straight lines. We should stand shoulder to shoulder and foot to foot. We should stand behind the *'Imām,* and face *Qiblah.*

The *'Imām* is the person who leads the *Ṣalāh*. When we offer *Ṣalāh* behind an *'Imām*, we should follow him. If we are not in the *Masjid* or at home, we can offer the *Ṣalāh* in any clean and quite place.

It is not compulsory for women to come to the *Masājid* ; they can pray at home or in the *Masjid*. Women can make their own *Jamā'ah*..

WE HAVE LEARNED:

- We must be clean before offering the *Ṣalāh*.
- We must offer *Ṣalāh* five times a day.
- We should offer *Ṣalāh* with the *Jamā'ah* and on time.

DO WE KNOW THESE WORDS?

Jamā'ah, *'Imām,* to please, in peace.

Lesson 18

THE FIVE DAILY *ṢALAWAT*

Allah ﷻ has asked us to pray five times a day. There are five daily *Farḍ* (obligatory) *Ṣalāh* each day. *Farḍ* means obligatory; something you have to do no matter what. *Farḍ* are actions which every Muslim is required to do for Allah ﷻ.

The first prayer of the day is called *Fajr*. *Fajr* prayer is made in the early morning. It is made after the first light of dawn and before the sunrise. The second prayer of the day is called *Ẓuhr*. *Ẓuhr* is offered right after noon time. We should not offer any prayer exactly at noon time.

The third prayer of the day is called *'Aṣr*. *'Aṣr* is offered in the afternoon. *'Aṣr* is offered when the sun is half way down from high noon.

The fourth prayer of the day is called *Maghrib*. *Maghrib* is offered right after sunset. The time of *Maghrib* does not last very long. We should make haste in offering *Maghrib*.

The last prayer of the day is called *'Isha'*. *'Isha'* is made when night has come.

If we miss a *Farḍ Ṣalāh* we must make it up as soon as possible. We offer five *Farḍ* prayers during the day and night. We start and end our day by praying to Allah ﷻ.

There are other prayers which are called *Sunnah, Wajib* and *Nafl*. We shall study them in Lesson 20. There is a special reward for the *Wajib*, *Sunnah* and *Nafl* prayers.

Allah ﷻ has fixed the time for each *Ṣalāh*. These times depend upon the movement of the earth around the sun. Nowadays it is easy to find the time of the *Ṣalāh* by looking at a watch. In Muslim societies one knows the time of *Ṣalāh* by hearing the *'Adhān*. In many places Islamic centers and *Masajid* publish a time table for the *Ṣalāh*. There are some watches and clocks available that could be timed for five daily *Ṣalawāt*.

We must always be a member of the *Masjid* and Islamic center in our neighborhood. We must always try to offer *Ṣalāh* in *Jamā'ah*. We must always take part in the activities of our *Masājid* and Islamic centers.

WE HAVE LEARNED:

- There are five daily *Farḍ* prayers at special times.
- The names of the five daily *Farḍ* prayers are: *Fajr*, *Ẓuhr*, *'Aṣr*, *Maghrib* and *'Ishā'*.
- We should offer daily *Farḍ* prayers in *Jamā'ah*.

DO WE KNOW THESE WORDS?

Fajr, *Ẓuhr*, *'Aṣr*, *Maghrib*, *'Ishā'*, *Farḍ*, member.

Lesson 19

MAKING THE INTENTION FOR THE *ṢALĀH*

Each *Ṣalāh* consists of offering two, three or four *Raka'āt*. A *Rak'ah* is a unit of *Ṣalāh*. To offer *Ṣalāh* we must make *Wuḍū*, stand on the *Sajjadah* in a clean place and face the *Qiblah*.

To make the intention, the *Niyyah,* for *Ṣalāh* is *Farḍ*. If there is no intention there is no *Ṣalāh*. Rasūlullāh ﷺ said:

إِنَّمَا الأَعْمَالُ بِالنِّيَّاتِ ...

" Indeed one's actions are decided by one's intention"
(Al-Bukhari)

A Muslim must always have good intentions. If we have good intentions, Allah ﷻ gives us reward for both the good intention and the good action.

Making the intention for *Ṣalāh* is very important for offering the prayers. In making the *Niyyah,* we must include the following things:

1. Our intention for offering *Ṣalāh* and the name of the *Ṣalāh*.
2. The number of *Raka'āt* and the kind of *Ṣalāh (Farḍ, Wajib, Sunnah, Nafl)*.
3. That it is for the sake of Allah ﷻ alone.
4. The direction of *Ka'bah.*
5. If we are following the *'Imām* or not.

For example, if we are offering two *Raka'āt* of *Sunnah* of *Fajr* we will make the following intention:

I intend to perform *Ṣalāh* of *Fajr,*
Two *Raka'āt Sunnah,*
For the sake of Allah ﷻ alone.
My face is turned towards the *Ka'bah.*

ṢALĀH اَلصَّلاة

اَللّٰهُ أَكْبَر

Intention for *Ṣalāh* Raise Hands Up to Ears and Say *"Allahu 'Akbar"*

Qiyām اَلْقِيَام

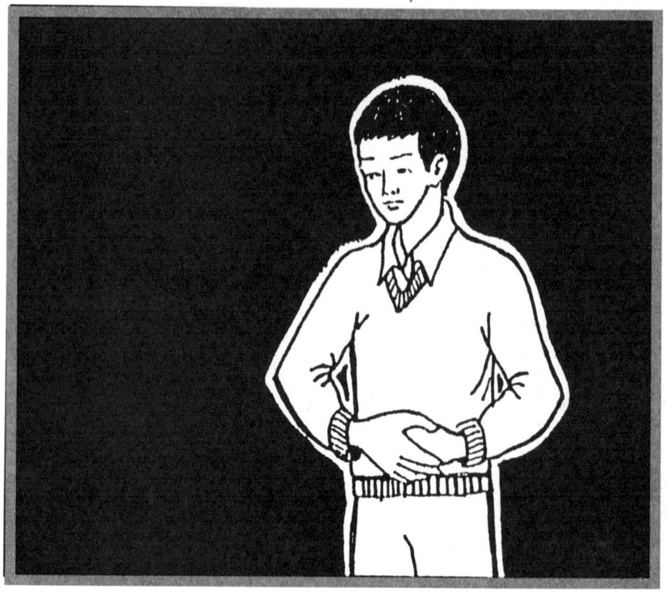

Rukū' الرُّكُوع

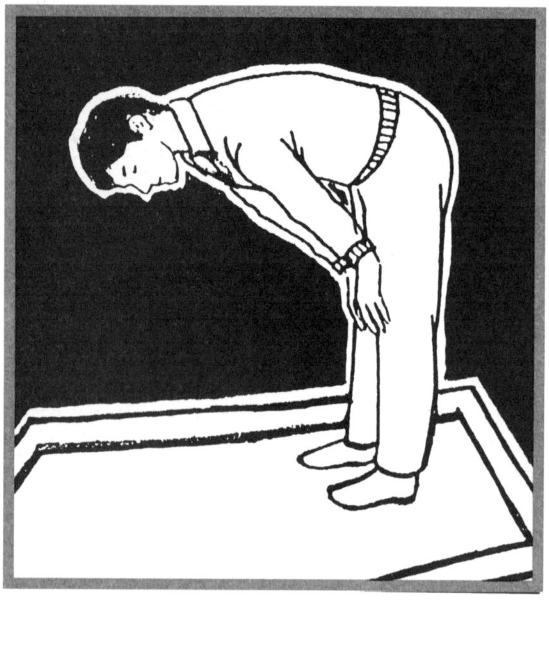

اَلْقَوْمَة

Qawmah

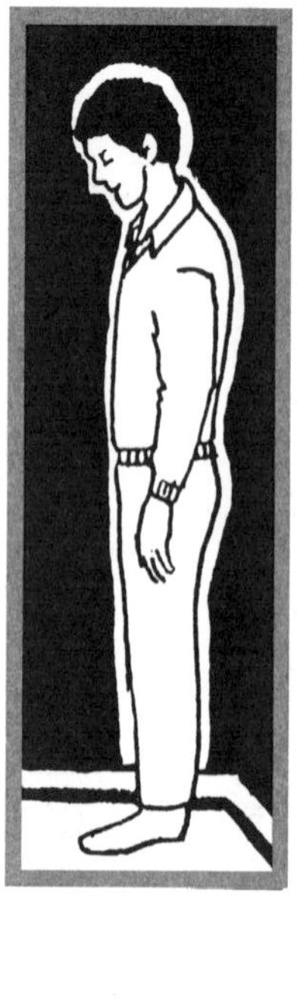

Sajdah السَّجْدَة

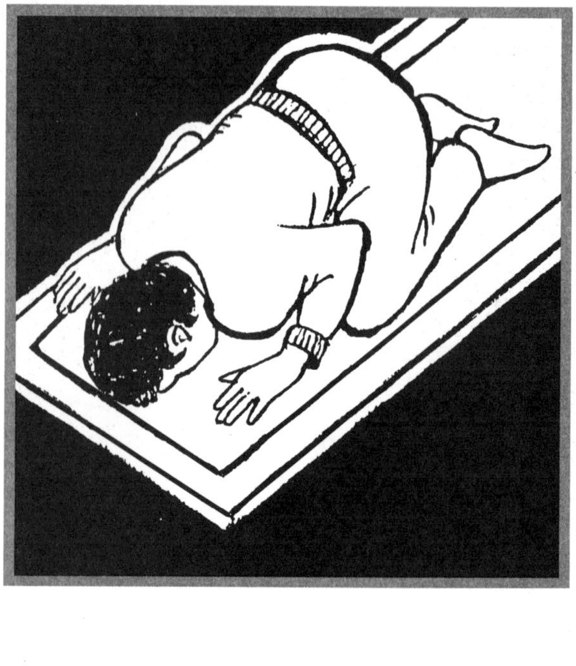

ṢALĀH اَلصَّلاة

Jalsah اَلْجَلْسَة

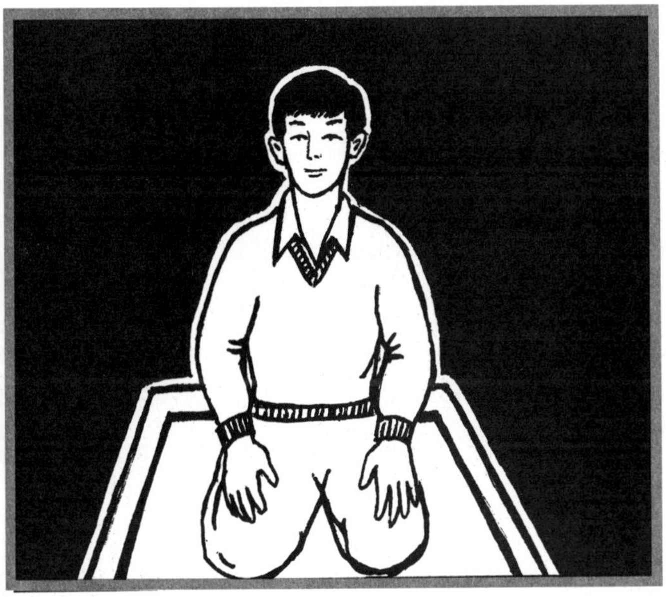

Taslīm-Turn FaceTowards Right

اَلتَّسْلِيمُ عَنِ الْيَمِين

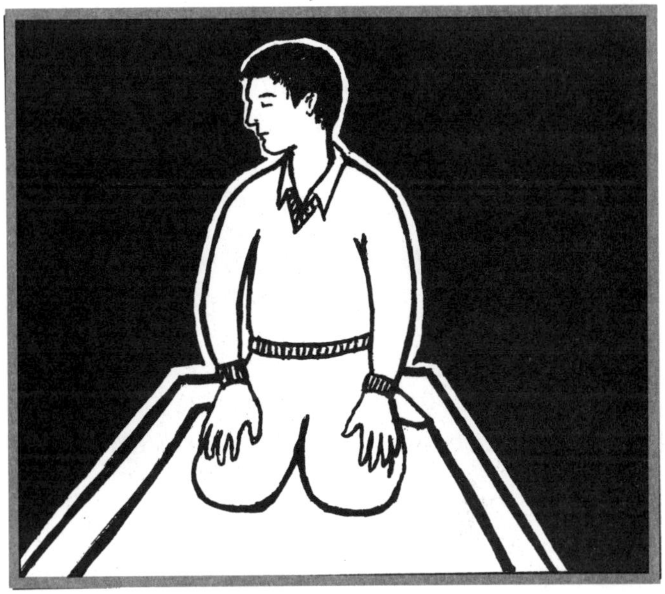

Taslīm-Turn Face Towards Left

اَلتَّسْلِيمُ عَنِ الشِّمَال

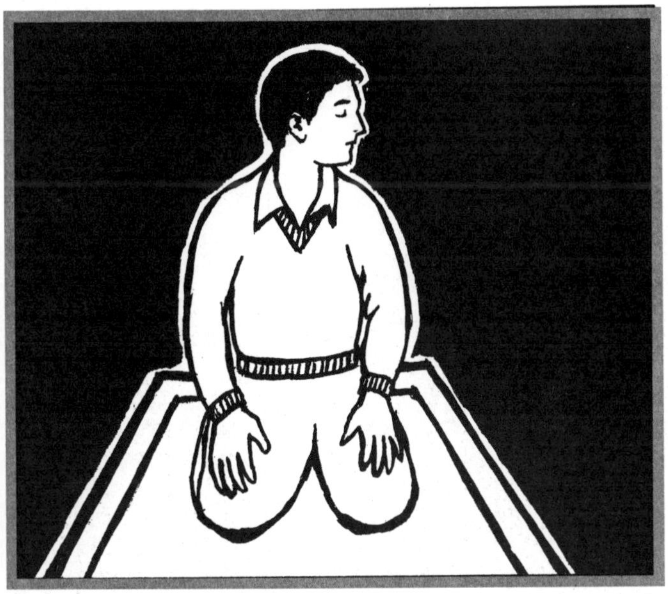

Du'ā' اَلدُّعاء

If we are offering two *Raka'āt Farḍ* of the *Fajr* with *Jamā'ah* we will say:

I intend to offer the *Ṣalāh* of *Fajr*.
Two *Raka'āt Farḍ*
For the sake of Allah ﷻ
My face is turned toward the *Ka'bah,*
Behind this *'Imām.*

When offering *Ṣalāh* in *Jamā'ah,* we wait for the *'Iqāmah* to be called. The *Mu'adhdhin* says the *'Iqāmah* and we line up for *Ṣalāh*. We stand shoulder to shoulder in straight lines behind the *'Imām.*

In the *Ṣalāh* of *Jamā'ah* we follow the *'Imām* and say what he says quietly, or we stand behind him quietly. When the *'Imām* reads the Qur'ān we must listen to him.

The *'Imām* starts the *Ṣalāh* by calling the *Takbīr, 'Allahu 'Akbar.*
This is called *Takbīr ut-Tahrīm,* the "*Takbīr* to Glorify Allah". Now we follow the *'Imām* step by step.

WE HAVE LEARNED:

- Making a *Niyyah* is a *Farḍ* for offering the *Ṣalāh,*
- Allah ﷻ accepts the actions of people according to their intentions.
- In offering the *Ṣalāh,* our intentions must be to obey and please Allah ﷻ alone.

DO WE KNOW THESE WORDS?

Niyyah, Qiblah, Rak'ah, Takbīr-ut-Taḥrīm.

SUGGESTED ACTIVITY:

Student must practice making the intention of various *Farḍ, Sunnah* and *Nafl Ṣalāh* with his or her teacher or parents.

Lesson 20

TYPES OF *ṢALAH*

Every *Ṣalāh* consists of units, called *Raka'āt*. Each *Rak'ah* is very much like the others, with small differences. Each *Ṣalāh* has two, three or four *Raka'āt*.

A *Ṣalāh* may be *Farḍ*, *Wājib*, *Sunnah* or *Nafl*. These differ from each other in their importance, the time we offer them and whether we do them alone or in *Jamā'ah*. But all of them have certain numbers of *Raka'āt* and all of them are offered the same way.

Farḍ means obligatory or compulsory. It is something we must do. Allah ﷻ has ordered the *Farḍ Ṣalawāt*. Not offering *Farḍ Ṣalāh* is a sin. The *Farḍ Ṣalawāt* are: *Fajr*, *Ẓuhr*, *'Aṣr*, *Maghrib* and *'Isha'*. All the *Farḍ Ṣalawāt* have their special times.

If we are not able to offer a *Farḍ Ṣalāh* on time we must perform it *Qaḍā'*. *Qaḍā'* means "making up". We must offer a "make up" as soon as we can. However, we should try very hard not to miss it in the first place.

Rasūlullāh ﷺ said:

اَلْعَهْدُ الَّذِي بَيْنَنَا وَبَيْنَهُمُ الصَّلاَةُ ، فَمَنْ تَرَكَهَا فَقَدْ كَفَرَ.

"The difference between a believer and a non-believer is the *Ṣalāh*".
This means a believer is one who offers his *Ṣalāh* on time.

Wājib *Ṣalāh* is also compulsory; *Wājib* means duty. It is also an obligation from Allah ﷻ, and the Prophet ﷺ always did it. It is next to *Farḍ* in its importance. *Witr* is a *Wājib Ṣalāh*; we will study *Witr Ṣalāh* after few lessons. *Jum'ah Ṣalāh* is *Wājib* (for men) every Friday at the time of *Ẓuhr* which it replaces. Also *Wājib* are the *Ṣalawāt* of the *'Id ul-Fitr* and *'Id ul-Aḍḥa*. *Jumu'ah* and the *Ṣalawāt* of *'Id* are also two *Raka'āt Ṣalawāt* prayed behind an *'Imām*. He gives a *Khutbah* (a special talk in two parts). The *Khutbah* is given before the *Ṣalāh* for *Jumu'ah* prayer and after the *Ṣalāh* in *'Eidain* prayers.

Sunnah Ṣalāh is not ordered by Allah ﷻ. It is the *Sunnah*, the practice, of Rasulullah ﷺ; it is what he did. He almost always prayed the *Ṣalawāt* we call *Sunnah*. Since we want to follow him, we should try to pray the *Sunnah Ṣalāh* as much as we can. *Sunnah Ṣalāh* may be offered with each *Farḍ Ṣalāh*; sometimes before *Farḍ*, some times after.

There are other special *Sunnah Ṣalawāt*, such as *Ṣalawāt* for rain and eclipses. We always join them if we can. The *Ṣalāt ut-Tarāwīḥ* during the month of *Ramaḍān* is *Sunnah*. It is preferably offered behind an *'Imām*, who is a *Ḥafiẓ* and recites part of the Qur'ān each night. The entire Qur'ān is generally completed during the month of *Ramaḍān*.

Nafl Ṣalāh is optional or voluntary. Rasūlullāh ﷺ offered even the *Nafl Ṣalāh* quite regularly. He told us that it is not compulsory for his *'Ummah*. However, there is a special reward from Allah ﷻ for offering *Nafl Ṣalāh*. There is no punishment for not offering *Nafl Ṣalāh*. We can offer *Nafl Ṣalāh* in groups of two *Raka'āt*, before or after the regular *Ṣalāh*.

There are also some special times for *Nafl Ṣalāh* such as after sunrise, in the late morning and when we feel grateful or especially thankful. We can offer *Nafl Ṣalāh* any time we like except after *Fajr* before sun rise and after *'Aṣr* before sunset; at those times there is no *Ṣalāh*.

WE HAVE LEARNED:

- The *Farḍ* and *Wājib Ṣalawāt* are required by Allah ﷻ.
- The *Sunnah Ṣalawāt* are offered following the *Sunnah* of the Prophet ﷺ.
- The *Nafl Ṣalawāt* are voluntary and we get extra *Thawāb* for offering them.

DO WE KNOW THESE WORDS?

Farḍ, *'Eidain*, *Nafl*, *Qaḍā'*, *Rak'ah* (singular), *Raka'āt* (plural), *Ṣalāh* or *Ṣalāt* (singular), *Ṣalawāt* (plural), *Sunnah*, *Tarāwīḥ*, *Thawāb*, *Witr*.

Lesson 21

PREPARING TO OFFER TWO *RAKA'AT FARḌ*

A *Ṣalāh* may have two, three or four *Raka'āt*. Every *Rak'ah* has many actions. All the *Raka'āt* have most actions in common. They differ from each other only slightly. The first and second *Raka'āt* are a pair. They go together. The third and fourth *Raka'āt* are a pair. Except for three *Farḍ Raka'āt* of *Maghrib* and three *Wājib Raka'āt* of *Witr,* all *Ṣalawāt* are offered in pairs of *Raka'āt*.

In the *Ṣalāh*, the Qur'ān is either recited out loud or said silently to oneself. This depends on which *Ṣalāh* is being performed. Silent *Ṣalāh* is called *Sirrī* (quiet). The *Sirrī Ṣalawāt* are *Ẓuhr* and *'Aṣr*.

Ṣalāh performed out loud is called *Jahrī* (audible). You must be able to hear the words with your ears. Only in the first two *Raka'āt* of *Jahri Ṣalāh* the Qur'ān is recited aloud. In the other two *Raka'āt* (*'Ishā'*) or one *Rak'ah* (*Maghrib*) the Qur'ān is recited silently. The *Jahrī Ṣalawāt* are *Fajr*, *Maghrib* and *'Ishā'*.

When you are in *Jamā'ah*, the *'Imām* will recite the Qur'ān aloud and you must listen. When he recites silently, you recite silently also or stand quietly. If you are alone, you can recite aloud or silently in the first two *Raka'āt*. This is true for both men and women.

As you know, we should always try to offer *Ṣalāh* with the *Jamā'ah*. For *Jamā'ah* we need an *'Imām* to lead. He should be the best person among us, or the oldest or wisest, or most learned (the one who knows the most Qur'ān).

The *'Imām* stands in front, with the men in rows behind him and the women in rows behind the men. If women are praying with women, the woman leading the *Ṣalāh* stands in the middle of the row. She may take one step forward or stay in the line. Those people who follow *'Imām* are called *Muqtadī*. *Muqtadī* means the follower.

Let us offer two *Raka'āt* of *Fajr Ṣalāh* in *Jamā'ah* behind an *'Imām*. As *Muqtadī*, we shall follow all the actions of the *'Imām*. The *Mu'adhdhin* says the *'Iqāmah* and the *Jamā'ah* lines up behind the *'Imām*. He raises his hands up to his ears. We hear him say, *"Allahu Akbar"*, the *Takbīr ut-Taḥrīm*. We raise our hands up to our ears and repeat, *"Allāhu Akbar"*.
The first *Rak'ah* has started.

WE HAVE LEARNED:

- *Raka'āt* are much alike, with a few differences. They usually come in pairs.
- Silent *Ṣalāh* is called *Sirrī*. In the *Jahri Ṣalāh,* the Qur'ān is recited out loud in the first two *Raka'āt*.
- When we are *Muqtadī* behind an *'Imām* we follow what he does.

DO WE KNOW THESE WORDS?

Sirrī, Jahrī, Muqtadī

Lesson 22

OFFERING TWO *RAKA'AT*: THE FIRST *RAK'AH*

First we make our intention; then, following the *'Imām*, we raise our hands up to the ears and say *Allāhu Akbar*. Boys put their hands over their navels, right hand over the left hand. Girls put their hands over their chests, right hand over the left hand.

These are the actions of the first *Rak'ah*:

1. *QIYAM:* STANDING

i) We stand up straight, facing the *Qiblah*, with our hands folded on navel or chest. We look at the place in front of us on the floor where our heads will touch. We keep our eyes focused there throughout the *Ṣalāh*.

ii) Recite Thanā' quietly (to recite Thanā' is not *Farḍ*).

Subhānaka 'Allahumma,	سُبْحَانَكَ اللَّهُمَّ
Wa bi-ḥamdi-ka	وَبِحَمْدِكَ ،
Wa tabāraka - 'smu-ka	وَتَبَارَكَ اسْمُكَ ،
Wa ta'ālā jaddu -ka	وَتَعَالَى جَدُّكَ ،
Wa la'ilāha ghairu-ka	وَلاَ إِلَهَ غَيْرُكَ

All Glory be to You, O Allah.
All praises are for You.
And Blessed is Your Name.
And exalted is Your Majesty.
And there is no deity except You

iii) The *'Imām* recites aloud *Tasmiyah* and *'Al-Fātihah:*

1. *Bismillah ir-Raḥmān ir-Raḥīm* بِسْمِ ٱللَّهِ ٱلرَّحْمَٰنِ ٱلرَّحِيمِ ﴿١﴾

2. *'Al-ḥamdu lillāhi Rabbil-'Ālamīn* ٱلْحَمْدُ لِلَّهِ رَبِّ ٱلْعَٰلَمِينَ ﴿٢﴾

3. *'Ar-Raḥmān ir-Raḥīm* ٱلرَّحْمَٰنِ ٱلرَّحِيمِ ﴿٣﴾

4. *Māliki yawmi-d-Dīn* مَٰلِكِ يَوْمِ ٱلدِّينِ ﴿٤﴾

5. *'Iyyāka na'budu wa iyyāka nasta'īn* إِيَّاكَ نَعْبُدُ وَإِيَّاكَ نَسْتَعِينُ ﴿٥﴾

6. *'Ihdinā-ṣ-ṣirāt-al mustaqīm* ٱهْدِنَا ٱلصِّرَٰطَ ٱلْمُسْتَقِيمَ ﴿٦﴾

7. *Ṣirāt-al-ladhīna 'an'amta 'alaihim* صِرَٰطَ ٱلَّذِينَ أَنْعَمْتَ عَلَيْهِمْ

Ghayril maghḍūbi 'alaihim غَيْرِ ٱلْمَغْضُوبِ عَلَيْهِمْ

Walā-ḍ-ḍāllīn. وَلَا ٱلضَّآلِّينَ ﴿٧﴾

1. In the name of Allah, Most Merciful, the Mercy Giving.
2. Praise be to Allah, Lord of the worlds.
3. Most Merciful, Most Kind.
4. Master of the Day of Judgment.
5. You alone we worship, You alone we ask for help.
6. Show us the Straight Path:
7. The path of those whom You have favored, Not (the path) of those who earn Your anger. Nor of those who go astray.

When the *'Imām* finishes reading *Sūrat ul-Fātiḥah,* we say *"Amīn"*.

iv) The *'Imām* recites a short *Sūrah* or three short *'Ayāt* of one long *Surah*. The *'Imām* in this example recites *Sūrat al-Kawthar*.

Bismillahi-r-Raḥmān-ir-Raḥīm بِسْمِ ٱللَّهِ ٱلرَّحْمَٰنِ ٱلرَّحِيمِ

1. *'Inna 'a'ṭaināka-l-Kawthar* إِنَّآ أَعْطَيْنَٰكَ ٱلْكَوْثَرَ ﴿١﴾

2. *Fa ṣalli li Rabbika wa-nḥar* فَصَلِّ لِرَبِّكَ وَٱنْحَرْ ﴿٢﴾

3. *'Inna shāni'aka huwa-l-'abtar* إِنَّ شَانِئَكَ هُوَ ٱلْأَبْتَرُ ﴿٣﴾

1. In the name of Allah, Most Merciful, the Mercy Giving
2. Indeed, to you (Muhammad) We have given the river of *al -Kawthar*
3. Therefore offer *Ṣalāh* to your Lord.
4. Indeed, he who is your enemy will be cut off.

2. RUKU' : BENDING DOWN

i) The *'Imām* says *"Allāhu 'Akbar"*, and makes a *Rukū'*, bowing from the waist, with his hands on his knees.

ii) Following the *'Imām*, we say *"Allāhu 'Akbar"* quietly and bow as well.

iii) We say *Tasbīḥ* of *Rukū'* silently (three times)

Subhāna Rabbi al-'Azīm (3 times) سُبْحَانَ رَبِّيَ الْعَظِيم
Glorious is my Lord, the Greatest.

3. *QAWMAH* : SHORT STANDING

i) The *'Imām* stands up saying:

Sami 'Allāhu li man ḥamidah سَمِعَ اللّٰهُ لِمَنْ حَمِدَه
Allah heard the call of the one who has praised Him.

ii) We answer the *'Imām*, saying:

Rabbanā wa-la-kāl-ḥamd رَبَّنَا وَلَكَ الْحَمْد
Our Lord the praise is for You.

4. FIRST *SAJDAH:* FIRST PROSTRATION

i) Raising his hands to his ears, the *'Imām* says *"Allāhu 'Akbar"* and goes into *Sajdah.*

ii) We follow, saying *"Allāhu 'Akbar"* quietly. Our knees, forehead and nose touch the floor; the palms of both hands are down touching the floor, placed next to the ears. The thumbs are in line with the lower lobes of the ears.

iii) We say *Tasbīḥ* of *Sajdah* three times, silently:

Subḥāna Rabbi al-'A'la (3 times) سُبْحَانَ رَبِّيَ الأَعْلَى
Glorious is my Lord, the Highest.

5. SHORT *JALSAH:* SHORT SITTING

i) The *'Imām* rises from *Sajdah*, saying *"Allahu 'Akbar"*, and sits briefly.

ii) We follow, saying *"Allahu 'Akbar"* quietly. We kneel on both knees sitting on our left foot which is tucked under; our right foot is propped up, resting on its toes.

iii) While sitting, we may silently say:

Rabbi 'ghfir lī wa li-wālidayya رَبِّ اغْفِرْ لِي وَلِوَالِدَيَّ
My Lord, forgive me, and my parents

6. SECOND *SAJDAH:* SECOND PROSTRATION

i) The *'Imām* says *"Allāhu 'Akbar"* and makes a second *Sajdah,* just like the first one.

ii) We follow, repeating *"Allāhu 'Akbar"* quietly.

iii) We repeat the *Tasbiḥ* of *Sajdah* silently, three times.

The *'Imām* says *"Allahu 'Akbar"* and rising from the second *Sajdah* stands up to complete the *Ṣalāh*. We follow the *'Imām* and stand up saying *"Allahu 'Akbar"*. The first *Rak'ah* is complete.

WE HAVE LEARNED:

- The actions of a *Rak'ah* are: *Qiyām, Rukū', Qawmah,* first *Sajdah,* short *Jalsah,* and second *Sajdah.*
- We say *"Allahu Akbar"* before every movement of the *Rak'ah* except coming up from *Rukū'* when we say *Sami' Allahu li-man ḥamidah* and *Rabbanā lakal ḥamd.*
- We listen to the *'Imām* when he recites and we follow him after he moves.

DO WE KNOW THESE WORDS?

Jalsah, Qawmah, Qiyām, Rukū', Sajdah, Tasmiyah

FURTHER HELP:

The *IQRA'* book ***Short Sūrahs*** will help you to learn more *Sūrahs* with their meaning and explanations.

Lesson 23

OFFERING TWO *RAKA'AT:* Completing the *Ṣalāh*

Having completed the first *Rak'ah*, we prepare to offer the second *Rak'ah*. The *'Imām* says *'Allahu 'Akbar* and rises for the second *Qiyām*. We also rise up, following the *'Imām* saying *'Allahu 'Akbar* quietly. Standing up completes the first *Rak'ah*.

Now the second *Rak'ah* starts.

1. *QIYĀM*: STANDING

The *'Imām* does not start the second *Rak'ah* with the *Thanā'*.
He starts with *Tasmiyah* and *Sūrat ul-Fātiḥah*.
He then recites another short *Sūrah* or *'Āyāt* from the Qur'ān .
Then he does the following as in the first *Rak'ah*:

2. *RUKU'*

3. *QAWMAH*

4. FIRST *SAJDAH*

5. SHORT *JALSAH*

6. SECOND SAJDAH

All of these are just like the first *Rak'ah*.

7. LONG *JALSAH*

In the second *Rak'ah*, after the second *Sajdah* we don't get up. We sit in a long *Jalsah* and recite the *'At - Tashahhud*, which is the statement of our best prayers and of what we as Muslims believe; *'As Salatu-l-*

'Ibrahimiyyah (Darud Ibrāhimi), which is wishing peace and blessings on the Prophet ﷺ; *Du'ā* and *Taslīm (salām).*

'At-Tashahhud:

'At-tahiyyātu li-Llāhi	اَلتَّحِيَّاتُ لِلَّهِ
Waṣ-ṣalawātu waṭ-ṭayyibātu	وَالصَّلَوَاتُ وَالطَّيِّبَاتِ ،
'As-salāmu 'alai-ka 'ayyuha-n-nabiyyu	اَلسَّلامُ عَلَيْكَ أَيُّهَا النَّبِيُّ
Wa raḥmatu-l-lāhi wa barakātu-Hu,	وَرَحْمَةُ اللهِ وَبَرَكَاتُهُ ،
'As-salāmu 'alainā	اَلسَّلامُ عَلَيْنَا
Wa 'ala 'ibādi-l-Lāhi-ṣ-ṣāliḥīn	وَعَلَى عِبَادِ اللهِ الصَّالِحِينَ ،
'Ashhadu 'an lā 'ilāha 'illa Llāhu	أَشْهَدُ أَنْ لاَ إِلَهَ إِلاَّ اللهُ ،
Wa 'ashhadu 'anna Muḥammadan	وَأَشْهَدُ أَنَّ مُحَمَّدًا
'Abdu-Hū wa rasūlū-Hu	عَبْدُهُ وَرَسُولُهُ .

All the praises, prayers and good things belong to Allah. O Prophet! Peace be upon you and His Mercy and His Blessings. Peace be upon us and upon the pious servants of Allah. I bear witness that there is no god but Allah and that Muhammad is His Servant and His Messenger.

When we come to *"'Ashhadu an..."* (the *Shahādah*) we raise our right index finger to bear witness that Allah ﷻ is One. And that Muhammad ﷺ is His Servant and Messenger.

After the *Shahādah,* we recite *Aṣ-Ṣalatu-l- 'Ibrahimiyyah (Darūd 'Ibrāhīmi)*

'Allahumma ṣalli 'alā Muḥammadin	اَللَّهُمَّ صَلِّ عَلَى مُحَمَّدٍ ،
Wa 'alā 'āli Muḥammadin	وَعَلَى آلِ مُحَمَّدٍ ،

Kamā ṣallaita ‘ala ’Ibrāhīma	كَمَا صَلَّيْتَ عَلَى إِبْرَاهِيمَ ،
Wa ‘ala ‘āli ’Ibrāhīma,	وَعَلَى آلِ إِبْرَاهِيمَ ،
’Inna-Ka Ḥamīdun Majīd	إِنَّكَ حَمِيدٌ مَجِيدٌ .
’Allāhumma bārik ’alā Muḥammadin	اَللَّهُمَّ بَارِكْ عَلَى مُحَمَّدٍ ،
Wa ’ala ‘āli Muḥammadin	وَعَلَى آلِ مُحَمَّدٍ ،
Kamā bārakta ‘ala ’Ibrāhīma	كَمَا بَارَكْتَ عَلَى إِبْرَاهِيمَ ،
Wa ‘ala ’āli ’Ibrāhima	وَعَلَى آلِ إِبْرَاهِيمَ ،
’Inna-Ka Ḥamīdun Majīd	إِنَّكَ حَمِيدٌ مَجِيدٌ .

O Allah, greet Muhammad and the family of Muhammad as You greeted Ibrahim and the family of Ibrahim, Indeed! You are the Glorious, Praised One.

O Allah, bless Muhammad and the family of Muhammad as you have blessed Ibrahim and the family of Ibrahim, Indeed! You are the Glorious, Praised One.

And finally we make a special *Du‘ā:*

’Allāhumma ’innī Ẓalamatu nafsī	اَللَّهُمَّ إِنِّي ظَلَمْتُ نَفْسِي
Ẓulman kathīran	ظُلْمًا كَثِيرًا ،
Wa la yaghfiru-dh-dhunūba ’illa ’anta,	وَلاَ يَغْفِرُ الذُّنُوبَ إِلاَّ أَنْتَ ،
Faghfir-lī maghfiratam min ‘indi-ka	فَاغْفِرْ لِي مَغْفِرَةً مِنْ عِنْدِكَ ،
Wa’r hamnī,	وَارْحَمْنِي ،
’Inna-Ka ’Anta-l-Ghafūru-r-Raḥīm	إِنَّكَ أَنْتَ الْغَفُورُ الرَّحِيمُ .

O Allah! I have done against myself great wrong and no one else can forgive sins except You. So forgive me and have mercy on me. Indeed! You are Forgiving, Merciful.

After saying *Du'ā*, the *'Imām* turns his face towards the right and says *Taslīm*:

'As-salāmu 'alaikum wa Raḥmatullāh اَلسَّلاَمُ عَلَيْكُمْ وَرَحْمَةُ اللّٰه ،
The Peace and Mercy of Allah be upon you.

Then he turns his face to the left and says:

'As-salāmu 'alaikum wa Raḥmatullāh اَلسَّلاَمُ عَلَيْكُمْ وَرَحْمَةُ اللّٰه ،
The Peace and Mercy of Allah be upon you.

We follow the *'Imām*, turning our faces first to the right, then to the left. We are greeting people on our right and left sides. We are greeting all the Muslims lined up on our right and left all the way around the world. We are greeting the Angels who are with us. This completes a two *Raka'āt Ṣalāh*.

WE HAVE LEARNED:

- At the end of the second *Rak'ah* there is a long *Jalsah*.
- In this *Jalsah* we recite *'At-Tashahhud, 'As-Salātu-l-Ibrāhimiyyah, Du'ā* and *Salām*
- We are wishing peace on the Prophet ﷺ, his family, all the Muslims and all the angels when we make our *Taslīm*.

DO WE KNOW THESE WORDS?

'At-Taḥiyyat, 'At-Tashahhud, 'Aṣ-Ṣalātul- Ibrāhimiyyah, Taslīm, blessings

Lesson 24

THE *FARḌ ṢALAWAT* OF FOUR *RAKA'AT*

The *Farḍ Ṣalawāt* of *Ẓuhr*, *'Aṣr* and *'Ishā'* have four *Raka'āt* each. We have now studied two *raka'āt*. We have completed a two *Raka'āt Ṣalāh*, *Ṣalātu-l-Fajr*.

If we intend to make a four *Raka'āt Ṣalāh*, we stand up after *'At-Tashahhud*. We will not recite *Ṣalātu-l-'Ibrahimiyyah* or *Taslīm*. We will leave these for the fourth *Rak'ah*.

The last two *Raka'āt* of four *Farḍ Ṣalawāt* are *Sirrī*, silent. Also we recite only *Sūratul-Fātiḥah;* no other *Sūrah* is recited in the last two *Raka'āt* of four *Rak'āt Farḍ Ṣalāh*.

Let's back up a little.

At the end of the second *Rak'ah*, the *'Imām* sits in *Jalsah* and reads only *'At-Tashahhud*. After saying the *Shahādah* with his index finger up, he says *'Allahu 'Akbar* and gets up.

He doesn't say anything else. We all say *'Allāhu 'Akbar* and rise also. We stand in *Qiyām* for the third *Rak'ah*. The *'Imām* completes the third and fourth *Raka'āt*. At the end of the fourth *Rak'ah* he sits in the long *Jalsah*. He completes the *Ṣalāh* by reciting *'At-Tashahhud*, *'Aṣ-Ṣalātu-l-'Ibrāhimiyyah* and *Taslīm*. The four *Raka'āt* of *Farḍ* are now completed.

We may then say *Tasbīhāt* and offer *Du'ā*. These *Tasbīhāt* may be three phrases that Prophet ﷺ advised us to say after every *Ṣalāh*. We say them 33 times each.

Subhān 'Allāh,	سُبْحَانَ الله ،	Glory be to Allah,
'Alḥamdu li-Llāh,	اَلْحَمْدُ لِلَّه ،	Praise be to Allah,
'Allāhu 'Akbar	اللَّهُ أَكْبَرُ	Allah is the Greatest.

We listen to the *'Imām*, follow him in *Tasbīhāt* and say, "*'Amīn*", when he says *Du'ā*. We can also offer *Farḍ Ṣalāh* without *Jamā'ah*. When we offer the *Farḍ Ṣalāh* alone we do exactly the same as the *'Imām* did.

WE HAVE LEARNED:

- The *Farḍ Ṣalawāt* of *Ẓuhr*, *'Aṣr* and *'Ishā'* have four *Raka'āt*.
- When praying four *Raka'āt*, we rise after saying the *Tashahhud* after the first two *Raka'āt*.
- The third and fourth *Raka'āt* are *Sirrī* (silent) and only *'Al-Fātiḥah* is recited silently.

DO WE KNOW THESE WORDS?

'Alḥamdu li-Llāh, 'Amīn, Tasbīḥāt, Subḥān Allāh.

Lesson 25

ṢALAT UL-WITR, SUNNAH AND *NAFL*

The *Ṣalāt ul-Witr* is *Wājib* and is offered without *Jamā'ah*. The *Ṣalāt-ul-Witr* may only be offered with *Jamā'ah* after the *Ṣalāh* of *Tarāwīḥ*. *Witr* means an odd number.

Ṣalāt ul-Witr must be made with an odd number of *Raka'āt*: 1,3,5,7,9,11, etc. There are three times when we can pray the *Ṣalāt ul-Witr*. The Prophet ﷺ from time to time prayed all three, though he usually performed *Ṣalāt ul-Witr* in the middle of the night. We can complete our *'Ishā'* prayer and pray three *Raka'āt* of *Witr*.

- We can pray *Ṣalāt ul-Witr* just before we go to sleep.
- We can pray in the middle of the night after *Ṣalāt ut-Tahajjud*.

There are also two ways to offer *Ṣalāt ul-Witr*. We can pray it in three *Raka'āt*, just like the *Ṣalāh* of *Maghrib*. Or, we can complete with *Taslīm*, any even number of *Raka'āt* 2, 4, 6, 8 etc. When we have completed any of the above number of *Raka'āt* we want, we add one *Rak'ah* of *Witr Ṣalāh*.

Now, while you are learning, you should pray *Witr* as your parents do or as your *'Imām* does. Later, you may decide that you would like to pray *Witr* differently. You may decide to pray in the middle of the night. Allah سبحانه وتعالى listens carefully and answers prayers which are offered in the middle of the night.

Whenever we offer it, *Ṣalāt ul-Witr* has one part different from the other *Ṣalawāt*. This is called the *Du'ā'* of *Qunūt*. After we read *Al-Fātiḥah* and a short *Sūrah,* we say *Takbīr* by raising our hands. Then we fold our hands again, right hand over left hand and recite *Du'ā* of *Qunūt* before we make *Rukū'*. We say the *Du'ā* of *Qunūt* silently.

'Allāhumma 'innā nasta'īnu-Ka	اَللَّهُمَّ إِنَّا نَسْتَعِينُكَ ،
Wa Nastaghfiru-Ka	وَنَسْتَغْفِرُكَ ،

Wa nu'minu bi-Ka	وَنُؤْمِنُ بِكَ ،
Wa natawakkalu 'alai-Ka	وَنَتَوَكَّلُ عَلَيْكَ ،
Wa nuthni 'alai-Ka-l-khaira	وَنُثْنِي عَلَيْكَ الْخَيْرَ ،
Wa nashkuru-Ka wa la nakfuru-Ka	وَنَشْكُرُكَ وَلاَ نَكْفُرُكَ ،
Wa nakhla'u wa natruku man yafjuru-Ka	وَنَخْلَعُ وَنَتْرُكُ مَنْ يَفْجُرُكَ .
'Allahumma 'Iyyā-Ka na'budu	اَللَّهُمَّ إِيَّاكَ نَعْبُدُ ،
Wa la-Ka nuṣallī wa nasjudu	وَلَكَ نُصَلِّي وَنَسْجُدُ ،
Wa 'ilai-Ka nas'ā wa naḥfidu	وَإِلَيْكَ نَسْعَى وَنَحْفِدُ ،
Wa narjū raḥmata-Ka	وَنَرْجُو رَحْمَتَكَ ،
Wa nakhshā 'adhaba-Ka	وَنَخْشَى عَذَابَكَ ،
'inna 'adhaba- Ka bill-kuffāri mulḥaq	إِنَّ عَذَابَكَ بِالْكُفَّارِ مُلْحَق .

Oh, Allah, we seek Your help, Your Guidance and Your Forgiveness. We believe in You and we have trust in You and we praise You in the best way.

And we thank You, and we do not deny you, And we turn away and give up the friendship of those who disobey You.

Oh, Allah, You alone we worship and for You alone we offer *Ṣalāh*, and to You alone we make *Sajdah*; and we make haste in turning to You, we hope for Your Mercy, and we fear Your Punishment. Indeed ! Your Punishment overtakes the *Kuffar*.

We could say another *Du'ā* instead of this one if we want.
Nafl and *Sunnah Ṣalawāt*, both two and four *Raka'āt*, are offered separately, usually without the *Jamā'ah*.

The *Sunnah Ṣalāh* of two *Raka'āt* is offered exactly the same as the *Farḍ*.

The *Sunnah Ṣalāh* of four *Raka'āt* is offered with only a small difference. In the third and fourth *Qiyām* we read *Tasmiyah, 'al-Fatiḥah* (like the *Farḍ Ṣalāh*) and a *Sūrah* or some *'Āyāt*.

Some *Sunnah Ṣalawāt* are offered with the *Jamā'ah*. The *Ṣalāt ut-Tarāwīḥ* in *Ramaḍān* and *Ṣalāt ul-'Eid* is a *Sunnah Ṣalāh* which we pray with *Jamā'ah*. We also usually pray the *Ṣalāt ul-Witr* with the *Jamā'ah* after *Ṣalāt ut-Tarāwīḥ*.

There are some other types of *Ṣalāh*, such as the funeral *Ṣalāh*. *Nafl Ṣalāh* is usually offered in pairs of two *Raka'āt, Sirrī*.

WE HAVE LEARNED:

- *Ṣalāt ul-Witr* has one, three, five, seven, or more odd-numbered *Raka'āt*.
- *Ṣalāt ul-Witr* has the *Du'ā* of *Qunūt* in it.
- The *Sunnah Ṣalawāt* are offered like the *Farḍ Ṣalāh*, but usually alone and usually *Sirrī*.

DO WE KNOW THESE WORDS?

Qunūt, disobey, make haste.

Lesson 26

HOW *ṢALAH* MUST BE OFFERED

Once the Messenger of Allah ﷻ entered the *Masjid.* A man came in soon after, offered the *Ṣalāh* and greeted Prophet Muhammad ﷺ. The Prophet ﷺ returned his greeting and said to him, "Go back and pray again, for you have not prayed."

The man offered the prayer again, came back and greeted Rasūlullāh ﷺ. He said to him, "Go back and pray again, for you have not prayed." The man offered the prayer again, came back and greeted Rasulullah ﷺ. He said to him again, "Go back and pray, for you have not prayed." The man said, "By Him Who has sent you with the Truth! I do not know a better way of praying. So kindly teach me how to pray."

The Prophet ﷺ said:

إِذَا قُمْتَ إِلَى الصَّلَاةِ فَكَبِّرْ ، ثُمَّ اقْرَأْ مَا تَيَسَّرَ مَعَكَ مِنَ الْقُرْآنِ ،
ثُمَّ ارْكَعْ حَتَّى تَطْمَئِنَّ رَاكِعًا ، ثُمَّ ارْفَعْ حَتَّى تَعْتَدِلَ قَائِمًا ،
ثُمَّ اسْجُدْ حَتَّى تَطْمَئِنَّ سَاجِدًا ، ثُمَّ ارْفَعْ حَتَّى تَطْمَئِنَّ جَالِسًا ،
وَافْعَلْ ذَلِكَ فِي صَلَاتِكَ كُلِّهَا .

(البخاري : باب ٩٥: حديث ٧٥٧)

"When you stand for the *Ṣalāh*, say *Takbīr* and then recite from the Qur'ān what you know, and then bow with calmness until you feel at ease, then rise from bowing till you stand straight. Afterwards, prostrate calmly till you feel at ease, and then rise and sit with calmness till you feel at ease, and then prostrate with calmness till you feel at ease in prostration, and do the same in the whole of your prayer."

Rasūlullāh ﷺ taught us that the *Ṣalāh* is a very special Blessing of Allah ﷻ. It must not be rushed into, but must be offered in peace and quiet. It must be offered properly and enjoyed fully.

We are busy all day long. We are doing this and that, running here and there. Our minds are full of words and ideas. Our eyes are full of pictures and images. Our hearts are busy trying to understand everything.

Sometimes we think we are too busy to stop and offer *Ṣalāh*. Nobody could be busier than the Prophet Muhammad ﷺ was. He was a father, husband, ruler, chief, counselor, *'Imām*, diplomat, judge, friend, advisor, teacher and carrier of the whole Qur'ān . He was responsible for everyone in the whole city. He was sent by Allah ﷻ for the entire Universe. Yet, he offered *Ṣalāh* more than anybody else. A busy person needs *Ṣalāh* even more than a relaxed person. When we stop what we are doing and make *Wuḍū'*, we refresh ourselves. When we stand for *Ṣalāh*, we stop thinking about ourselves for a while.

We pray in a very relaxed manner. We don't hurry, wiggle, or throw our bodies around. We don't poke our neighbor or look to see what he or she is doing. We don't scratch, giggle or fix our clothes.

The *Ṣalāh* is quiet and sweet and it puts quietness and sweetness in our lives. If we have done anything wrong, the *Ṣalāh* cleans us of it. The Prophet Muhammad ﷺ said *Ṣalāh* is like washing in a river outside our door five times a day. Would we be clean?

A wise man said that all things in life are just to fill up time between the *Ṣalawāt*. The *Ṣalāh*, remembering our Creator, is what really matters.

We have studied many details now; you have a lot of new words and are trying to understand times of *Ṣalāh*, number of *Raka'āt Farḍ*, *Sunnah* and *Nafl*. You will learn more about the *Ṣalāh* at junior and senior levels. You will learn all of this with practice. It is easy after you do it for a time.

But the most important thing is to remember this main point:
***Ṣalāh* is our responsibility to Allah ﷻ.**
Through *Ṣalāh* we show our love to Him.
Through *Ṣalāh* we remember our connection to Him.
Through *Ṣalāh* we remember that whatever is happening, He is the Greatest.
Ṣalāh puts us on His team. It keeps us straight and strong.

So take this responsibility, your parents and teachers will help you, but it is yours now. It is a duty and a big blessing for the rest of your life.

WE HAVE LEARNED:

- *Ṣalāh* must be offered in peace and relaxed manner.
- *Ṣalāh* puts quiteness and sweetness into our lives.
- *Ṣalāh* is our respponsibility to Allah ﷻ.

DO WE KNOW THESE WORDS?

greeting, diplomat, counsellor, advisor, relaxed

Lesson 27

MAKING FRIENDS

Rasūlullāh ﷺ advised us to always choose the company of good people. He said:

اَلْمَرْءُ عَلَى دِينِ خَلِيلِهِ ، فَلْيَنْظُرْ أَحَدُكُمْ مَنْ يُخَالِلُ

"People usually follow the ways of their friends; everyone must judge a person by the company he keeps."
(Transmitted by Abū Dāwūd)

The Qur'ān also advises us:

يَٰٓأَيُّهَا ٱلَّذِينَ ءَامَنُوا۟ ٱتَّقُوا۟ ٱللَّهَ وَكُونُوا۟ مَعَ ٱلصَّٰدِقِينَ

O Believers be careful to your duty to Allah and
Be with the truthful people.
(*'At-Tawbah* 9:119)

It is natural for us to be like the people we live, play and work with. When we are in the company of good friends and righteous people we always think and talk about good things. We can do many good things with our friends, such as fundraising, or helping neighbors.

In the same way, people who spend their time in the company of people who like to get in trouble will one day get in trouble themselves. Many young people begin to smoke or take drugs if their friends are taking them. Some of them begin to steal and fight.

Friends who think and behave badly often will not care if they hurt people who love and care for them. If one of their friends becomes successful in something or gains some benefit, they may become jealous. Jealousy is a problem. The person who has jealousy in his or her heart will do anything to take away the happiness of the person he or she does not like. We ask Allah ﷻ to protect us from anyone who is jealous of us. We also ask Allah ﷻ to keep jealousy out of our hearts.

For that reason, no matter how strong we are in our faith and character, we should not take chances with our life in this world or the next. We must also know that *Shaiṭān* is waiting to lead us to the wrong way. The Qur'ān warns us:

أَلَمْ أَعْهَدْ إِلَيْكُمْ يَٰبَنِىٓ ءَادَمَ أَن لَّا تَعْبُدُوا۟ ٱلشَّيْطَٰنَ ۖ
إِنَّهُۥ لَكُمْ عَدُوٌّ مُّبِينٌ

"Children of Adam, did I not tell you that you should not serve *Shaiṭān*? Certainly he is your enemy!"
(*Yā-Sīn* 36:60)

Shaiṭān is our enemy. He loves to whisper bad thoughts into our hearts and put wrong ideas into our minds. Sometimes we act on these thoughts and do things which we should not do. In acting on *Shaiṭān's* whisper we disobey Allah ﷻ and His Messenger ﷺ. We can also hurt ourselves and even hurt others.

We must ask Allah's Help to keep *Shaiṭān's* whispers away from us. One way to do this is to always say:

أَعُوذُ بِاللَّهِ مِنَ الشَّيْطَانِ الرَّجِيمِ

'A'udhu bī-llāhi min ash-Shaiṭān ir-Rajīm
(I seek refuge in Allah from the Cursed *Shaiṭān*)

The best thing for us to do is to follow the Qur'ān and the *Sunnah* of Rasūlullāh ﷺ. We should also keep the company of the good people.

WE HAVE LEARNED

- All Muslims should stay in the company of the righteous and avoid the company of people who follow the wrong actions.
- *Shaiṭān* wants to lead all human beings to the wrong path.
- We must seek Allah's Protection from *Shaiṭān's* whispers.

DO WE KNOW THESE WORDS?

Straight Path, whispers, misguide, jealousy, protect, righteous

Lesson 28

THE RIGHTS THE QUR'AN HAS OVER US

The Qur'ān is the Word of Allah ﷻ. It is a very special Book. Therefore we must treat it with respect and care. The Qur'ān has many rights over us.

The first right the Qur'ān has over us is that we be clean before we pick it up to read. Allah ﷻ says in the Qur'ān:

لَّا يَمَسُّهُۥٓ إِلَّا ٱلْمُطَهَّرُونَ

"No one should touch it the Qur'ān except those
who are pure and clean."
(*Al-Wāqi'ah*:79)

Before we pick up the Qur'ān to read, we must make a complete *Wuḍū'*. In this way we prepare ourselves to read the Words of Allah ﷻ by showing respect to the Qur'ān.

Another way of showing our love and respect for the Qur'ān is to read it each day as much as we can. When we sit to read the Qur'ān we should do so in a quiet and clean place. It is important to read it with *Tartīl. Tartīl* means that we should say each word with the proper pronunciation. If we do not recite the words of the Qur'ān properly, we can change their meanings.

Whenever we hear others reciting the Qur'ān, we must listen quietly. Allah ﷻ says:

وَإِذَا قُرِئَ ٱلْقُرْءَانُ فَٱسْتَمِعُوا۟ لَهُۥ وَأَنصِتُوا۟ لَعَلَّكُمْ تُرْحَمُونَ

"When the Qur'ān is recited, listen to it and be silent
that you might receive mercy."
(*Al-'Araf* 7:204)

It is very disrespectful for us to talk or play while the Qur'ān is being recited.

In addition to reading the Qur'ān and listening to it being recited, it is important for us to understand what its words mean. There are many translations of the Qur'ān into English. Some *'Ayāt* (verses) may be difficult for us to understand when we are little. It is good to ask our parents, our *'Imām* or our Islamic Studies teachers if they can help explain any *'Ayāt* we do not understand.

The final thing we can do to show that we love and respect the Qur'ān is to follow what it tells us to do. In this way we show that we truly love this gift from our Creator, Allah ﷻ!

We must encourage our parents and elders to help all the schools which teach the Qur'ān. We must do the same when we grow up. All these are the ways by which we show our love and respect for the Qur'ān.

WE HAVE LEARNED

- We treat the Qur'ān with great respect.
- We must make *Wuḍū* before we touch and read the Qur'ān.
- We should follow the teachings of the Qur'ān.
- We should support the schools which teach the Qur'ān.

WE KNOW THESE WORDS?

Practice, attention, *Tartīl,* pronunciation, translations

Lesson 29

THE RIGHTS OF OUR PARENTS

Allah ﷻ says in the Qur'ān:

وَقَضَىٰ رَبُّكَ أَلَّا تَعْبُدُوٓا۟ إِلَّآ إِيَّاهُ وَبِٱلْوَٰلِدَيْنِ إِحْسَٰنًا ۚ

And your Lord commands you to worship none other except
Him and that you be kind to parents.
(*Al-'Isrā'* 17:23)

In this *'Ayah* Allah ﷻ teaches us two very important things: First, we must worship only Him and, second, we must always be kind to our parents. Allah ﷻ tells us that the value of our parents is next to worshiping Him. This shows us how important it is to love and help our parents.

Our parents do their best to take care of us. They teach us good manners and care for our happiness and comfort. We must always show respect for our mothers and fathers. They spend their money, time and whole lives trying to make things easy for us. They make sure that we have food and a safe, comfortable homes. When we need help in anything, they're always there to help us.

We must always show respect to our mothers and fathers. We must never talk back to them, even if they tell us something we do not want to hear because they are trying to do their best for us.

We can never repay the love and help our parents give us. But one way to show our thankfulness is to help them, especially when they become old and cannot do the things they used to do when they were younger. As we grow older our parents grow older too.

When they get older, they become weaker and may get sick more often. They need the same care and love from their children that they gave to them when their children were young.

When we grow up we will take jobs, get married and have our own children. We may move away from our parents and live in our own homes. But as we grow older we must never forget our parents. They may need our help much more when they get very old and it is our duty to help them the best we can. If they do not want to live alone, we should make a special place for them in our home. This way we can be close to them all the time so we can love and care for them.

We should always pray for our parents. After our parents have left this life, we should continue to pray that Allah ﷻ accepts them into *Jannah*.

Here are some of the ways in which we can show love and respect to our parents:

- Greet them every day by saying *'As-Salamu 'Alaīkum* as we wake up from sleep or come back home from school.
- Help them in doing chores around the house.
- Smile at them, say good things and, most important, sit and talk to them when they are relaxing.
- Buy them presents on special occasions.
- Take good care of them, especially when they are sick.
- When we start working, share our money with them.

We should always pray for our parents. We should ask our parents to remember us in their *Du'ā'*. Rasūlullāh ﷺ said that,

> "There are three types of prayers that are always answered: the prayers of an oppressed person, the prayers of a traveler, and the prayers of parents for their children."
> (Abū Dāwūd, Tirmidhī, Ibn Mājah)

WE HAVE LEARNED

- We treat our parents with all our love and respect.
- Our parents spend their lives caring for us.
- We must take care of our parents when they grow old.

DO WE KNOW THESE WORDS?

Value, comfort, patient, continue

Lesson 30

GOOD MANNERS TOWARDS ALL

As Muslims we must always try our best to follow the way of Rasūlullāh ﷺ. Allah ﷻ describes him in the *Qur'ān*:

لَّقَدْ كَانَ لَكُمْ فِي رَسُولِ ٱللَّهِ أُسْوَةٌ حَسَنَةٌ ...

Indeed there is for you in the example of Rasūlullāh ﷺ a beautiful pattern.
(*Al-Aḥzāb* 33:21)

Allah ﷻ also says to the Prophet ﷺ in the Qur'ān:

وَإِنَّكَ لَعَلَىٰ خُلُقٍ عَظِيمٍ

"Certainly, you are of the highest character."
(*Al-Qalam* 68:4)

Rasūlullāh ﷺ said that the people with the best manners will be closest to him on the Day of Judgment. If we show good manners towards everyone, we will be good representatives of Islam. People will come to respect us and respect our faith. If we behave improperly, then people may think badly about us and our faith.

Rasūlullāh ﷺ treated everybody with kindness and respect. He spoke kindly and never used harsh words. He was forgiving to those who fought him. He was a generous person and gave away every thing he received.

In Madinah there were Jewish and Christian people. Rasūlullāh ﷺ always treated them nicely. He respected their laws, customs and religion. When a dispute came to him involving the People of the Book (the Jews and Christians), Rasūlullāh ﷺ always judged it fairly, even if the judgment was against the Muslims.

We must follow Rasūlullāh ﷺ. We must respect everyone and treat them with fairness. We must never be unfair to people because of their religion, color, language and culture.

Rasūlullāh ﷺ was sent as *Raḥmat Lil-'Alamīn* (a Mercy to all the Worlds.) Once the *Ṣaḥābah* came to Rasūlullāh ﷺ and asked him to curse the idol-worshippers of Makkah. But Rasūlullāh ﷺ replied:

إِنِّي لَمْ أُبْعَثْ لَعَّانًا ، وَلَكِنْ بُعِثْتُ رَحْمَةً

"I was not sent to curse people, but to be a mercy for all."
(Muslim)

Allah ﷻ gave every human being certain rights. We must respect those rights. Some ways we can do this are:

- Always be kind to people and show them respect.
- Never think badly about anyone.
- Always be helpful towards those who need help.
- Always share with our friends and neighbors.
- Never say or do anything that would hurt other people.

Islam is a religion of peace and friendship. A Muslim must always try to spread peace between people. Allah ﷻ and His Prophet ﷺ love those people who establish peace in their homes, neighborhoods, communities, nations and the world. Rasūlullāh ﷺ told us to:

أَفْشُوا السَّلامَ بَيْنَكُمْ تَحَابُّوا.

"Spread peace among yourselves, for then you will love each other."
(Abū Dāwūd, Ibn Mājah)

WE HAVE LEARNED

- Muslims must follow the beautiful example of Rasūlullāh ﷺ.
- We must be merciful to all humanity, animals and environment.
- We must treat everyone with respect and kindness.

DO WE KNOW THESE WORDS?

Created, character, representatives, offend, curse

Lesson 31

PROTECTING OUR EARTH

Allah ﷻ has blessed us by putting us on this planet, Earth. In fact, Allah ﷻ created Earth and then created human beings to be His *Khalifah* (representative) over it. He commanded us to be in charge of the planet and all that is on it.

However, we must remember that we are to take care of our planet and all that is on it. It does not belong to us and we have to treat it that way. Allah ﷻ tells us in the Qur'ān that:

وَلِلَّهِ مَا فِي ٱلسَّمَٰوَٰتِ وَمَا فِي ٱلْأَرْضِ
وَكَانَ ٱللَّهُ بِكُلِّ شَيْءٍ مُّحِيطًا

"To Allah belongs all that is in the heavens and in the earth, for God encompasses everything."
(*An-Nisā'* 4:126)

Because the planet does not belong to us, we have to protect it and make sure that we do not ruin it. These days many people waste a lot of things that Allah ﷻ has given us on Earth. We cut down trees without replacing them with new trees; we throw away paper, glass, and metal when they could be recycled and used again.

The resources of our Earth are limited. This means that once we use them all up, there is no more. For example, if we cut down all the trees to make paper, furniture, and houses without planting new trees, there will come a time when there will be no more trees. This would be very bad for the whole planet. Trees give many things to humans and animals, including oxygen. If all the trees were used up, the Earth would slowly turn into a desert. It would then be very difficult for us to live.

We also must be careful not to pollute the land, air, and water. Rasūlullāh ﷺ

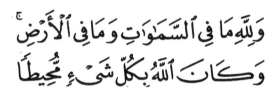

said that being clean is a very important part of being a Muslim. This does not only mean having a clean body, clean clothes or a clean house. It also means making sure the environment around us is clean. If we see garbage in our parks or forests we should stop and pick it up. We can join with our community to help keep the environment clean. We must join with all the people in our neighborhoods, towns, cities, and nation to work together to protect our planet.

If we treat the Earth with love and respect, it will continue to give us the resources we need to live, *in-shā'-Allah!*

WE HAVE LEARNED

- All of creation belongs to Allah ﷻ.
- Allah ﷻ made us His vicegerents to look after the Earth.
- We must not waste the resources that the Earth gives us.

DO WE KNOW THESE WORDS?

Resources, pollute, *Khalīfah*, recycle, environment, community

APPENDIX - 1 TWO SHORT *SURAHS*

SURAT AL-IKHLAṢ (THE SINCERITY), 112:1-4

Bismillāhi-r-Raḥmān-Ir-Raḥīm.

بِسۡمِ ٱللَّهِ ٱلرَّحۡمَٰنِ ٱلرَّحِيمِ

1. *Qul Huwa-'Allāhu 'Aḥad,*

قُلۡ هُوَ ٱللَّهُ أَحَدٌ ١

2. *'Allāhu-ṣ-Ṣamad.*

ٱللَّهُ ٱلصَّمَدُ ٢

3. *Lam-yalid wa lam-yūlad.*

لَمۡ يَلِدۡ وَلَمۡ يُولَدۡ ٣

4. *Wa lam yukul-la-Hu kufuwan 'aḥad.*

وَلَمۡ يَكُن لَّهُۥ كُفُوًا أَحَدٌۢ ٤

In the name of Allah, Most-Kind, Most Merciful.
1. Say: He is Allah, the One.
2. Allah the Eternal,
3. He does not give birth (to anyone); nor did anyone give birth to Him.
4. And there is no one equal to Him.

SURAT AL-'AṢR (THE TIME), 103:1-3

Bismillah ir-Rahman ir-Rahīm

بِسۡمِ ٱللَّهِ ٱلرَّحۡمَٰنِ ٱلرَّحِيمِ

1. *Wa-l-'Aṣr.*

وَٱلۡعَصۡرِ ١

2. *'Inna-l-'insāna lafī khusr.*

إِنَّ ٱلۡإِنسَٰنَ لَفِي خُسۡرٍ ٢

3. *'Illa-lladhina 'āmanū Wa 'amilū-ṣ-ṣāliḥāti, wa tawāṣaw bi-l-ḥaqqi wa tawāṣaw bi-ṣ-ṣabr.*

إِلَّا ٱلَّذِينَ ءَامَنُواْ وَعَمِلُواْ ٱلصَّٰلِحَٰتِ
وَتَوَاصَوۡاْ بِٱلۡحَقِّ وَتَوَاصَوۡاْ بِٱلصَّبۡرِ ٣

In the name of Allah, Most-Kind, Most Merciful.
1. By the Time,
2. Indeed! Man is at a loss;
3. Except those who have faith, and do good works, encourage one another to truth and encourage one another to patience.

APPENDIX - II

CHART OF *RAKA'AT* OF EACH *ṢALĀH*

Let us read about the number of *Rak'āt* for each of the daily prayer.

Fajr, the Morning Prayer has:
Two *Raka'āt* of *Sunnah*
Two *Raka'āt* of *Farḍ*

Ẓuhr, the Early Noon prayer has:
Four *Raka'āt* of *Sunnah*
Four *Raka'āt* of *Farḍ*
Four *Raka'āt* of *Sunnah*

'Aṣr, the Afternoon Prayer has:
Four *Raka'āt* of *Sunnah*
Four *Raka'āt* of *Farḍ*

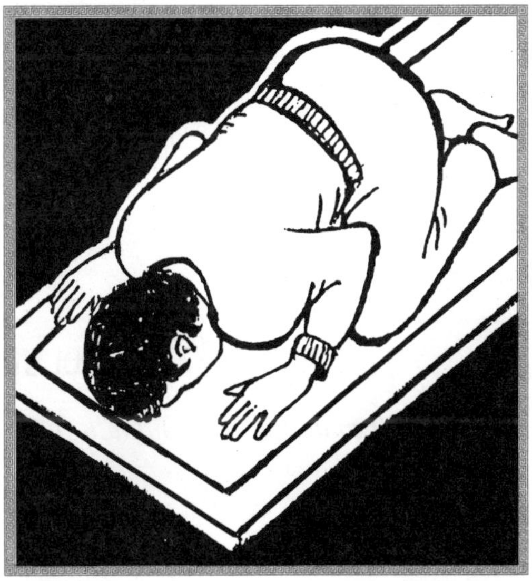

Maghrib, the Evening Prayer has:
Three *Raka'āt* of *Farḍ*
Two *Raka'āt* of *Sunnah*

'Ishā', the Night Prayer has:
Four *Raka'āt* of *Sunnah*
Four *Raka'āt* of *Farḍ*
Two *Raka'āt* of *Sunnah*
Three *Raka'āt* of *Witr*

APPENDIX - III *AD'IYAH:* ENTERING AND LEAVING MASJID

* ***DU'A'*: ENTERING THE *MASJID*** *

اَللّٰهُمَّ افْتَحْ لِي أَبْوَابَ رَحْمَتِكَ.

'Allāhumma ftaḥ lī 'abwāba raḥmati-ka

* *

O Allah! Open the doors of your *Rahmah* (Mercy) for me

* * *

* ***DU'A'*: LEAVING THE *MASJID*** *

اَللّٰهُمَّ إِنِّي أَسْأَلُكَ مِنْ فَضْلِكَ.

'Allāhumma 'innī 'as'alu-ka min faḍli-ka

* *

O Allah! I ask you to give me Your *Fadl* (Bounties).

* * *

APPENDIX - IV SOME *TASBIHAT* AFTER THE *ṢALĀH*

أَسْتَغْفِرُ اللّٰهَ الْعَظِيمَ الَّذِي لاَ إِلَهَ إِلاَّ هُوَ وَأَتُوبُ إِلَيْه .

´Astaghfiru-llaha-l-´aẓīma-lladhī la ´ilaha illa huwa wa ´atūbu' ´ilaih

* *

I seek forgiveness from Allah, the Almighty, there is no other god except Him, and I repent to Him.

* * *.

لاَ إِلَهَ إِلاَّ أَنْتَ ، سُبْحَانَكَ إِنِّي كُنْتُ مِنَ الظَّالِمِينَ .

La ´ilaha ´illa ´anta, subhana-ka ´innī kuntu mina-ẓ-ẓālimīn

* *

There is no God but You, glory be to You, O God, surely Iwas from among the wrong doers

* * *

سُبْحَانَ اللّٰهِ، وَالْحَمْدُ لِلّٰهِ ، وَلاَ إِلَهَ إِلاَّ اللّٰهُ ، وَاللّٰهُ أَكْبَر.

Subḥānallāhī, wa-l-ḥamdu li-Llāhi, wa-lā ´ilāha ´illa-Llāhu, wa-Llāhu' akbar

* *

Glory be to Allah, praise be to Allah, there is no god but Allah, and Allah is the Greatest.

* * *

حَسْبُنَا اللّٰهُ وَنِعْمَ الْوَكِيل

Ḥasbunā-Llāhu wa-ni'ma-l-wakīl

* *

God is sufficient for us, and He is the best Guardian

* *

اَللّٰهُمَّ أَنْتَ السَّلاَمُ ، وَمِنْكَ السَّلاَمُ ، وَإِلَيْكَ يَرْجِعُ السَّلاَمَ ، فَحَيِّنَا رَبَّنَا بِالسَّلاَمِ ، وَأَدْخِلْنَا دَارَ السَّلامِ ، تَبَارَكْتَ يَا ذَا الْجَلاَلِ وَالإِكْرَامِ.

'Allāhumma 'anta-s-salām wa minka-s-salām wa 'ilai-ka yarji'u-s-salām ḥayyaina rabban'a bis-salām wa 'adkhilna dara-s-salām. Tabārakta yā dha-l-jalāli wa-l-'ikrām

* *

O Allah! You are peace, and from You comes peace, blessed are You, o Lord of all glory and honor.

* * *

اَللّٰهُمَّ أَنْتَ عَفُوٌّ تُحِبُّ الْعَفْوَ ، فَاعْفُ عَنِّي.

'Allāhumma 'anta 'afuwwun tuḥibbu-l-'afwa fa'fu 'anni

* *

O Allah! You are Most Forgiving, and love forgiveness, so forgive me.

رَبِّ اغْفِرْ لِي وَلِوَالِدَيَّ وَلِلْمُؤْمِنِينَ يَوْمَ يَقُومُ الْحِسَابُ.

Rabbi-ghfir lī wa-li-wālidāyya wa-lil-mu'minīna yawma yaqūmu-l-ḥisāb

* *

My lord! Pardon me and my parents and the believers on the Day of Judgment.

* * *

اَللّٰهُمَّ اغْفِرْ لِي وَارْحَمْنِي وَاهْدِنِي وَعَافِنِي وَارْزُقْنِي.

'Allahumma 'ighfir lī wa-rḥamnī wa-hdinī, wa 'afinī wa rzuqnī

* *

O Allah! Forgive me, have mercy upon me, give me guidance, give me health, and provide for means of my living.

* * *

اَللّٰهُمَّ أَعِنَّا عَلَى ذِكْرِكَ وَشُكْرِكَ وَحُسْنِ عِبَادَتِك.

'Allahumma 'a'innā 'alā dhikri-ka wa-shukrīka wa-ḥusni 'ibādati-ka

* *

O Allah! Help us to remember You, thank You, and perform worship to You.

* * *

رَبَّنَا آتِنَا فِي الدُّنْيَا حَسَنَةً وَفِي الآخِرَةِ حَسَنَةً وَقِنَا عَذَابَ النَّار.

Rabbanā 'atinā fi-d-dunyā ḥasanatan wa-fi-l-'ākhirati ḥasanatan wa-qinā 'adhāba-n-nār

* *

O our Lord! Give us good reward in this world, and a good reward in the Hereafter, and protect us from the torment of the Hell-fire.

* * *

رَبَّنَا تَقَبَّلْ مِنَّا إِنَّكَ أَنْتَ السَّمِيعُ الْعَلِيمُ.

Rabbanā taqabbal minnā 'inna-ka 'anta-s-samī 'u-l-'alīm

* *

O our Lord! Do accept from us (our good deeds). Indeed You are the All-Hearing, the All-Knowing.

APPENDIX - VI SIX *KALIMAT* OF MUSLIM FAITH

FIRST *KALIMAH:* *AT - ṬAYYIBAH* اَلطَّيِّبَة (The PURITY)

لاَ إِلَهَ إِلاَّ اللّهُ ، مُحَمَّدٌ رَسُولُ اللّهِ.

Lā ʻilāha illa-Llāhu Muḥammadun Rasūlullāh

* *

There is no god but Allah, Muhammad is the Messenger of Allah.

* * *

SECOND *KALIMAH:* *ASH - SHAHADAH* اَلشَّهَادَة (The WITNESS)

أَشْهَدُ أَنْ لاَ إِلَهَ إِلاَّ اللّهُ ، وَحْدَهُ لاَ شَرِيكَ لَهُ ، وَأَشْهَدُ أَنَّ مُحَمَّدًا عَبْدُهُ وَرَسُولُه.

'Ashhadu an lā ilāha 'illā Llahu waḥda-hu lā sharīka la-hu
Wa-'ashhadu 'anna Muḥammadan ʻabdu-hu wa-rasūlu-hu

* *

I bear witness that there is no god but Allah, He is only One and has no partner with Him and I bear witness that Muhammad is His Servant and His Messenger

* * *

THIRD *KALIMAH:* *AT - TAMJID* اَلتَّمْجِيد (THE EXALTATION)

سُبْحَانَ اللّهِ ، وَالْحَمْدُ لِلّهِ ، وَلاَ إِلَهَ إِلاَّ اللّهُ ، وَاللّهُ أَكْبَرُ ،
وَلاَ حَوْلَ وَلاَ قُوَّةَ إِلاَّ بِاللهِ الْعَلِيِّ الْعَظِيم.

Subḥana allāhi wa-lḥamdu li-llāhi wa-lā ilāha 'illā Allahu wa-llahu
'Akbar wa-la ḥawlā wa-lā quwwata 'illa bi-Llahi ʻaliyyī-l-ʻazīm

* * *

Allah is glorified, praise is due to Allah; no one is worthy of worship but Allah; He is the Greatest; there is no power and no strength, but by the Help of Allah, the Highest, the Most Sublime.

* * *

FOURTH *KALIMAH:* *AT - TAWHID* اَلتَّوحِيد (THE UNITY)

لاَ إِلَهَ إِلاَّ اللّهُ ، وَحْدَهُ لاَ شَرِيكَ لَهُ ، لَهُ الْمُلْكُ ، وَلَهُ الْحَمْدُ ، يُحْيِي وَيُمِيتُ ،
وَهُوَ حَيٌّ لاَ يَمُوتُ أَبَدًا، ذُو الْجَلاَلِ وَالإِكْرَامِ ، بِيَدِهِ الْخَيْرُ ، وَهُوَ عَلَى كُلِّ شَيْءٍ قَدِير.

Lā 'ilāha 'illa allāhu waḥda-hu lā sharīka la-hu la-hu-l-mulku wa-la-hu-l-ḥamdu; yuḥyī wa-yumītu wa-huwa ḥayyun lā yamūtu ʼabadan;dhul jalali-wa-l-' ikrām; bīyadihi-l-khairu wa-huwa ʻala kulli shai'in qadīr

* * *

There is no god but Allah, He is One, He has no partner with Him only He is the Ruler (of heavens and earth), and only to Him is due all praise. Only Allah has the power to bring everything into life, and to cause death, and He is Everliving and will never die. Allah is the Possessor of all Greatness, honor, and Reverence. All goodness is in His Hands, and He has the Power to do everything.

* * *

FIFTH *KALIMAH:* *AL - ISTIGHFĀR* الإِسْتِغْفَارُ (FORGIVENESS)

أَسْتَغْفِرُ اللّٰهَ رَبِّي مِنْ كُلِّ ذَنْبٍ أَذْنَبْتُهُ ، عَمْدًا أَوْ خَطَأً ، سِرًّا أَوْ عَلاَنِيَةً ،
وَأَتُوبُ إِلَيْهِ مِنَ الذَّنْبِ الَّذِي أَعْلَمُ ، إِنَّكَ أَنْتَ عَلاَّمُ الْغُيُوبِ ،
وَسَتَّارُ الْعُيُوبِ ، وَغَفَّارُ الذُّنُوبِ ، وَلاَ حَوْلَ وَلاَ قُوَّةَ إِلاَّ بِاللّٰهِ الْعَلِيِّ الْعَظِيمِ.

'Astaghfiru Allāha Rabbī min kulli dhanbin 'adhnabtu-hu 'amadan 'aw khata'an sirran 'aw 'alānīyatan wa 'atūbu ilai-hi mina-dh-dhanbi-lladhī 'allamu; 'innaka 'anta 'allamu-l-ghuyūbi wa sattāru-l-'uyūbi wa-ghaffāru-dh-dhunūbi wa-lā ḥawla wa-lā quwwata 'illa bi-Llāhi-l-'aliyyī-l-'azīm

* *

I ask the Fogiveness of Allah, my Lord, from every sin which I have committed consciously or unconsciously, hidden or openly. I (also) ask His Forgiveness from the sins which I know or those which I do not know. Indeed, You (Allah) are the Knower of all things which are hidden from human beings, and you are the concealer of our defects and shortcomings. And You are the Forgiver of all sins. And there is no power and no strength but by the help of Allah, the Most High, the Most Sublime.

* * *

SIXTH *KALIMAH:* *RADDUL KUFR* رَدُّ الْكُفْرِ REFUTATION OF THE *KUFR*

اللَّهُمَّ إِنِّي أَعُوذُ بِكَ مِنْ أَنْ أُشْرِكَ بِكَ شَيْئًا وَأَنَا أَعْلَمُ ، وَأَسْتَغْفِرُكَ لِمَا لاَ أَعْلَمُ بِهِ وَتُبْتُ عَنْهُ ،
وَتَبَرَّأْتُ مِنَ الْكُفْرِ وَالشِّرْكِ وَالْكَذِبِ وَالْغِيبَةِ وَالْبِدْعَةِ وَالنَّمِيمَةِ وَالْفَوَاحِشِ
وَالْبُهْتَانِ وَالْمَعَاصِي كُلِّهَا ، وَأَسْلَمْتُ وَأَقُولُ : لاَ إِلَهَ إِلاَّ اللَّهُ ، مُحَمَّدٌ رَسُولُ اللَّهِ

'Allahumma 'innī 'a'ūdhu bi-ka min' an' ushrika bi-ka shai'an wa-'ana a'lamu bihi wa-'astaghfiru-ka limā lā 'a'lamu bi-hi wa tubtu 'an-hu wa-tabarratu min-l-kufri wa-sh-shirki wa-l- kadhībi wa-l-ghīb ati wa-l-bid ati wa-nnamīmati wa-l-fawḥishi wa-l-buhtīni wa-l-ma'āṣī kulli-ha wa-'aslamtu wa-'aqūlu lā 'ilaha 'illā Llāhu Muhammadun Rasūllūh

* *

O Allah! I seek Your Refuge wherein to be saved from all kinds of *Shirk* that I know. Also ask Your Forgiveness from all the sins which I do not know. I sincerely ask Your Forgiveness from all my previous sins, and I disassociate myself from *Kufr* (disbelief) *Shirk* (polytheism) lies, backbiting, heresy, talebearing, all shameful deeds, and false accusations and every kind of disobedience. I accept Islam, and I say, there is no god but Allah, Muhammad is His Messenger

* * *

For more *'Ad'iyah* see our book:

* OUR BOOK OF *DU'A'* by Fadel Abdallah

Vocabulary

'Alḥamdu li-Llāh	Praise be to Allah.
'Al-Kawthar	Abundance, name of a special river in Paradise.
'Al-Qiyāmah	The Day of Judgment.
'Āmīn	May Allah accept; it is said after *Du'ā*.
Angels	Creations of Allah ﷻ made from light.
'Arkān	Pillars.
'Aṣr	Afternoon, the *Ṣalāh* of afternoon.
'Aslama	To Surrender, to submit, to commit oneself to the Will of God.
'Aṣ-Ṣirāt	The path, the Straight Path of Islam.
'Aṣ-Ṣūr	A special trumpet to be blown by Angel *'Israfīl* to call people to wake up and gather for the Day of Judgment.
'At-Taḥiyyāt	Saying a greeting on the Prophet ﷺ through reciting a special *Du'ā'*.
'At-Tashahhud	To bear witness that Allah ﷻ is one and Muhammad ﷺ is His messenger. We say: *'Ashhadu 'an-lā llāha ill-Allāhu wa 'Ashhadu 'anna Muhammadan Rasūlullāh.*
Blessings	A gift of Allah's favor; that which makes one happy.
Character	A combination of qualities of an individual.
Command	To order with authority.
Complete	Having all needed parts or elements; lacking nothing; whole.
Condition	The state in which a person or thing exists.
Deputy	One person appointed to act for another.
Discharge	To unload; to perform or fulfill a function.

Discipline	Systematic training; order.
Disobey	To refuse to obey.
Darud 'Ibrahimi	Wishing peace and blessings on the Prophet ﷺ by reciting a special *Ṣalāh*.
Essential	Very important.
Establish	To setup; to make firm.
Eternal	Having neither beginning or end; everlasting.
Fajr	Dawn; the *Ṣalāh* of *Fajr*
Farā'id	Plural of *Farḍ*.
Farḍ	Obligatory, something that must be done.
Guidance	The act of guiding, showing path.
'Ibādah	Worship.
'Imām	The leader, leader of the prayer.
'Imān	Faith.
'Imān Mufaṣṣal	Comprehensive faith.
'Injīl	The book given to Prophet 'Isa ﷺ (Jesus).
Intention	Plan to do something; purpose
Intercession	Praying for others, recommending others.
'Iqāmah	A second call for prayer before the obligatory *Ṣalāh*.
'Ishā'	Night, the *Ṣalāh* of *'Ishā'*.
'Isrāfīl	Name of the angel who will blow the *Ṣūr,* or trumpet.
'Izra'īl	The angel who takes our souls away and causes us to die.
Jahrī	Said out loud, audible, opposite of *Sirrī*.
Jalsah	Short sitting between two prostrations.
Jamā'ah	Congregation, group.
Ja' Namaz	Prayer rug (Persian word for *Sajjadah*).

Khalīfah	Successor; Deputy ; Vicegerent.
Kirāman Kātibīn	Honorific title of the angles that record human deeds.
The Last Day	End of the world, new beginning.
Maghrib	Sunset, the *Ṣalāh* of *Maghrib.*
Make haste	Rush to do something.
Masḥ	Wiping with wet hands.
Member	Person belonging to a group.
Message	Some news sent to someone.
Mīkā'īl	Name of the angel whose duty is to arrange for rainfall and supply provisions to the creations of Allah ﷻ, with His Command.
Mu'adhdhin	The person who called *('Adhān)* for prayers.
Munkir	Name of one of the two angels who will question the dead.
Muqtadī	The one who follows the *'Imām* in a *Ṣalāh.*
Nabī	A prophet.
Najāsah	Uncleanliness, state of impurity.
Nakīr	Name of one of the two angels who will question the dead.
Niyyah	Intention.
Nostrils	The two openings of the nose.
Nūr	Light.
Obedience	Doing what one is asked to do.
Peace	A state of no war or agitation.
Permission	Letting someone do something.
Praiseworthy	Someone who is liked by others.
Prophets	Messengers of Allah ﷻ.

Pillars	Support.
Purify	To make clean; without any sin.
Qaḍā'	Making up for a missed prayer.
Qa'dah	Sitting after prostration in second *Rak'ah* or in the last *Rak'ah.*
Qadar	Divine decree, destiny, Power of Allah ﷻ.
Qawmah	Short standing in a *Ṣalāh.*
Qiblah	Direction of *Ka'bah* to where Muslims face in prayer.
Qiyām	Standing up after prostration in *Ṣalāh.*
Qunūt	A special kind of *Du'ā'* recited in *Ṣalāt ul-Witr.*
Rasūl	A messenger.
Rak'ah	A unit of *Ṣalāh, Raka'āt* (plural).
Record	Writing of facts and things which took place.
Regular	Made according to rules; orderly.
Recover	To get something after losing it.
Rinse	To wash with water.
Rukū'	Bending down in *Ṣalāh.*
Sajdah	Prostration in *Ṣalāh.*
Sajjadah	Prayer rug.
Ṣalāh	Prayer, *Ṣalawāt* (plural).
Salima	To be safe and sound; to be at peace.
Shafā'ah	Intercession, recommendation.
Sirrī	Silent, opposite of *Jahrī.*
Soul	Part of us which is close to Allah ﷻ.
Spirit	An important part of us, we can not see but know it is within us.
Specific	Something clear and definite.

Subḥān-Allah	Glory be to Allah.
Ṣuḥuf	Scriptures, singular *Ṣaḥīfah.*
Sunnah	Tradition as practised by the Prophet, prayers that are not *Farḍ.*
Ṭahārah	Purity, state of being pure, opposite of *Najāsah.*
Ṭāhir	Pure, clean.
Tarāwīḥ	A special *Sunnah Ṣalāh* during the month of Ramaḍān.
Tasbīḥāt	Saying: *"Ṣubḥanallah, Alhamdulillah, Allahu Akabar"* after finishing *Ṣalāh.*
Taslīm	Saying: *"'Assalamu 'alaikum wa-Raḥmatullah"* to the end of *Ṣalāh.*
Tasmiyah	Saying: *Bismillahi-r-Raḥmāni-r-Rahīm.*
Tayammum	Ablution for prayer when water is not available.
Tawrāh	*Torah,* the book revealed to Prophet Moses عليه السلام.
To bear witness	To see or know something personally and tell others about it.
To please	To make one happy.
Tortured	To hurt and cause pain to someone.
'Ulamā'	Learned men, religious scholars.
'Ummah	Community; Nation.
Vicegerent	Someone who acts in place of an important person; the deputy.
Waḥī	Revelation, the Message of Allah to His Prophets.
Witr	A *Sunnah Ṣalāh.*
Worship	Pray to someone.
Zabūr	The scripture revealed to Prophet Dāwūd عليه السلام.
Ẓuhr	Noon, *Ṣalāh* of *Ẓuhr.*

Introducing the Authors

Dr. Abidullah Ghazi, Executive Director of IQRA'International, and his wife Dr. Tasneema Ghazi, Director of Curriculum, are co-founder of IQRA' International Educational Foundation (a non-profit Islamic Educational Trust) and Chief Editors of its educational program. They have combined their talents and expertise and dedicated their lives to produce a Comprehensive Program of Islamic Studies for our children and youth and to develop IQRA' into a major center of research and development for Islamic Studies, specializing in Islamic education.

Abidullah Ghazi, M.A. (Alig.), M.Sc. Econ. (LSE London), Ph.D. (Harvard)

Dr. Abidullah Ghazi, a specialist in Islamic Studies and Comparative Religion, belongs to a prominent family of the *'Ulama'* of India. His family has been active in the field of Islamic education, *Da'wah,* and struggle for freedom from British imperialism. Dr. Ghazi's early education was carried in traditional Madaris including Dar ul-'Ulum (Deoband, India), and Qasim ul-'Ulum (Faqirwali, Pakistan). He has studied at Muslim University, Aligarh. The London School of Economics, and Harvard University. He has taught at the Universities of Jamia Millia Islamia, Delhi, London, Harvard, San Diego, Minnesota, Northwestern, Governors State and King Abdul Aziz University, Jeddah. He is a consultant for the development of the program of Islamic Studies in various schools and universities. He is a well-known writer, community worker, speaker and poet.

Tasneema K. Ghazi, M.A. (Alig.), M.Ed. (Allahabad), Acd. Dip. (London), CAGS (Harvard), Ph.D. (Minnesota)

Mrs. Ghazi is a specialist in Child Development and Reading (Curriculum and Instruction). She has studied at the Universities of Aligarh, Allahabad, London, Harvard, San Diego and Minnesota. She has taught in India, England, Jeddah, and the United States at various levels: kindergarten, elementary, junior, senior and university. Since her arrival in USA in 1968, she has been involved with the schools of Islamic Studies providing them valuable advice and guidance. Working with children is her main interest.

Dr. Ghazi have a life-long commitment to write, develop and produce Islamic educational material and quality textbooks at various levels.

جل جلاله